'At a time when faith schools in the UK are once aga[in in the] educational debate, this book serves to add to the con[versation,] the reader that an exploration of faith schools in pra[ctice is] important, and it helps us to understand these complex and diverse school communities.'

Dr Helena Miller, Director of Research and Evaluation, UJIA

'This well-researched book provides useful information, inquiries, and insights into the intense efforts of Muslim and Jewish schools to maintain both their religious identity and wider community engagement in the face of whimsical government policies on multiculturalism and extremism. This is compulsory reading for policy makers in education.'

Dr Musharraf Hussain Al Azhari OBE, CEO and Chief Imam, Karimia Institute

Reaching In, Reaching Out

Reaching In, Reaching Out

Faith schools, community engagement and 21st-century skills for intercultural understanding

Marie Parker-Jenkins, Meli Glenn, and Jan Germen Janmaat

Institute of Education Press

First published in 2014 by the Institute of Education, University of London,
20 Bedford Way, London WC1H 0AL
ioepress.co.uk

© Marie Parker-Jenkins, Meli Glenn, and Jan Germen Janmaat 2015

British Library Cataloguing in Publication Data:
A catalogue record for this publication is available from the British Library

ISBNs
978-1-78277-024-4 (paperback)
978-1-78277-081-7 (PDF eBook)
978-1-78277-082-4 (ePub eBook)
978-1-78277-083-1 (Kindle eBook)

All rights reserved. No part of this publication may be reproduced, stored in a retrieval system, or transmitted in any form or by any means, electronic, mechanical, photocopying, recording, or otherwise, without the prior permission of the copyright owner.

Every effort has been made to trace copyright holders and to obtain their permission for the use of copyright material. The publisher apologizes for any errors or omissions and would be grateful if notified of any corrections that should be incorporated in future reprints or editions of this book.

The opinions expressed in this publication are those of the authors and do not necessarily reflect the views of the Institute of Education, University of London.

Typeset by Quadrant Infotech (India) Pvt Ltd
Printed by CPI Group (UK) Ltd, Croydon CR0 4YY

Cover design by emc design ltd

Contents

Glossary	viii
Acknowledgements	xii
About the authors	xiii
Introduction: The context of learning	1
1 Faith schools: Historical and legal background	17
2 Faith schools and the wider community: Controversy and debate	33
3 Jewish perspectives and concepts of community	49
4 Muslim perspectives and concepts of community	65
5 Skills for engagement	83
Conclusion: Where reaching starts and stops	96
Bibliography	113
Index	137

Glossary

Academies	State schools directly funded by central government via the Department for Education, and independent of direct control from local government. Most are registered as charities and may receive additional support from sponsors.
Aqidah	The unfaltering belief in Allah and everything related to him.
Alienation	A sociological concept developed by classical theorists such as Durkheim. Refers to a low degree of integration and a high degree of distance or isolation, sometimes as a deliberate act to maintain identity.
Ashkenazi Jews	Jews of Central and Eastern European descent.
AMS	Association of Muslim Schools. A UK membership organization for Muslim schools that provides teacher training, school inspection under the supervision of Ofsted, and consultancy services.
'Big Society'	Flagship policy of the UK Conservative Party that places emphasis on people and communities with notions of autonomy, strong civil society, and providing for oneself.
BDBJ	The Board of Deputies of British Jews.
Community schools	Schools that are state-funded and run by local authorities, which control the school building and land, admissions, and staff recruitment.
Community cohesion	Promotion of greater knowledge, respect, and contact between groups within the community, and developing a greater sense of citizenship.
Cultural sustainability	Passing on traditions, customs, and values through the family and the extent to which it is possible to carry this out in a non-Jewish or non-Muslim society.

Glossary

DCSF	Department for Children, Schools and Families (2007–10), responsible for all issues affecting young people up to the age of 19.
DfE	Department for Education (2010 – to date), preceded by the DCSF.
Engagement	Ability or willingness of different communities to live, work, and study alongside, and with, other communities.
Eruv	Area enclosed by a wire boundary symbolically extending the private domain of Jewish households into public areas.
Faith schools	Educational institutions that aspire to inculcate religious beliefs within children and perpetuate a particular lifestyle.
Free schools	State-funded schools run by parents, teachers, charities, and businesses on a non-profit basis. Free to attend and not controlled by local government. Set up in 2010 and an extension of the Academies programme.
Hijab	Headscarf or covering worn by Muslim women and young girls.
The Holy Qur'an	Central text of Islam which was revealed to the Prophet Mohammad
Independent schools	Fee-paying schools that are independent of some of the regulations applying to state-funded schools.
Imam	A leader of a Muslim community. Imam in Shia Islam is reserved for 12 direct descendants of Mohammed who are credited with the highest knowledge and piety. Commonly used in the British context to refer to mosque imams who lead prayers, teach children reading the Arabic Quran, and lead different religious rituals, e.g. marriages, funerals, births, etc.

Kehilla	The organisation of a Jewish population for communal and charitable purposes.
LBC	Leo Baeck College, providing training for educators and rabbis for liberal, progressive Judaism.
Madrassahs	Supplementary schools of Islamic education often operating in a mosque or community centre and usually outside of the compulsory school day.
Maslaks	Muslim denominations, e.g. Deobandi and Barelvi, including Shia.
Millah	In Islam, a community or group sharing the same religion and common traditions.
Multiculturalism	The recognition of group difference based on such characteristics as culture, religion, and language, and reflected in legislation and policy.
Ofsted	Office for Standards in Education, the UK national government body responsible for the inspection of schools in England and Wales.
Pikuach	UK Jewish school inspection service – the statutory equivalent to Ofsted – established in 1996 and led by the Board of Deputies to inspect and monitor Jewish religious education.
Qahal	Hebrew for assembly or congregation.
Rabbi	Religious leader of a Jewish community.
Sephardi Jews	Jews descended from the Near East and the Iberian Peninsula.
Shia Muslims	The second largest denomination of Islam and followers of Ali as the Prophet Mohammed's successor.
Sunni Muslims	The largest faction of Islam and followers of Abu Bakr as the Prophet Mohammed's successor.
Talmud	Central text of Rabbinic Judaism, considered second to the Torah, containing the oral law of Judaism.
Taqwa	Obedience to Allah and the laws of Islam.

Glossary

Torah	The central document of Judaism and the first five books of the Bible.
Ummah	Arabic word for community or nation that refers to the collective community of Muslims around the world. Tawhid (oneness of God), risalah (prophethood), and akhuwah (brotherhood) are the foundational principles of Muslim ummah.
Voluntary aided schools	State-funded schools in which the governing body owns the building, employs the staff, and sets the admission criteria. Most voluntary aided schools are faith schools.

Acknowledgements

Our research for this book has involved discussion and correspondence with a large number of people who all played a role in providing us with invaluable information and guidance. We would like to acknowledge a number of individuals and organizations in particular.

We conducted research in several faith schools. They were representative of Jewish and Muslim schools which we will not name here, to ensure anonymity, but to whom we extend our thanks in this general address. Respondents in these schools spoke openly, with a shared interest in fostering greater understanding of their faith group.

We also wish to acknowledge the assistance of organizations supportive of our work, namely: the Leo Baeck Centre for Jewish Education; United Synagogues of Britain; the Board of Deputies of British Jews; Liberal Reform Progressive Synagogues; and the Association of Muslim Schools, UK. These organizations acted as important 'gatekeepers', helping us ensure access to schools within the different faith traditions and navigating cultural sensitivities.

We are also grateful to Jim Collins and Nicole Edmonson of IOE Press for their ongoing support of the book; to Louise Spry of Nottingham Trent University for helping with our preparation of the application for funding; and to the Economic and Social Research Council (ESRC) for granting us a research award. Thanks to research assistants Huma Shantu, Dr Manny O'Grady, Miriam Shindler, and Elise Burton for their help with editing, data collection, and literature searches. Thanks also go to Brigete Clancy of the University of Limerick for her transcription of interviews from our case study. Invaluable reviewers who also provided important guidance and feedback in earlier drafts of this manuscript are: Professor Mark Halstead, University of Huddersfield; Dr Saeeda Shah, University of Leicester; Dr Sean McLoughlin, University of Leeds; Dr Musharraf Hussain OBE, chair of the Christian Muslim Forum; Rapahal Zarum, London School of Jewish Studies; Dr Helena Miller, Director of Research and Evaluation at the United Jewish Israel Appeal; Dr Sadif Rizvi of The Open University; and Dr Helen Everett of the National Foundation for Educational Research.

While a number of people and organizations have thus been consulted over the issues contained in the book, the opinions expressed are entirely our own, likewise any errors or omissions.

About the authors

Marie Parker-Jenkins is Professor of Education at the Department of Education and Professional Studies, and Director of the Research Centre for Education and Professional Practice, at the University of Limerick. Her research focuses on issues of social justice, human rights, and ethnicity. She has worked in Bermuda, Canada, and Australia, taught in seven universities, and assumed positions as visiting professor and academic scholar at McGill University, Canada; James Cooke University, Australia; Uppsala University, Sweden; and the University of Warwick, UK. She has also provided workshops on such subjects as citizenship, community, and personal identity. Her last co-authored book was *Education that Matters: Critical pedagogy and development education at local and global level*. Her previous books include *Aiming High: Raising the attainment of pupils from culturally diverse backgrounds*; *In Good Faith: Schools, religion and public funding*, and *Children of Islam: Meeting the educational needs of Muslim children*.

Meli Glenn is an education consultant with over ten years' experience in educational research, teacher training, and education innovation. Her work and interests focus on the intersection between education technology and emerging markets. She currently serves as a non-executive director and strategic advisor for a number of education technology start-up companies across Europe, Asia, and Africa. Some of her clients include the Department for International Development, the European Union, the British Council, and the National College for Leadership of Schools and Children's services. She previously worked with Pearson and the Institute of Education, University of London. She also has experience leading development workshops on teaching methodology and innovative curricula in Haiti, Guinea, India, and Benin.

Jan Germen Janmaat is Reader of Comparative Social Science at the Centre for Learning and Life Chances in Knowledge Economies and Societies (LLAKES), Institute of Education, University of London. He teaches on the MA in Comparative Education and has developed a keen awareness of issues of inequality, competition, and diversity in education systems and their effects on civic attitudes and social cohesion more generally. This has resulted in a series of articles published in journals as diverse as *Ethnic and Racial Studies, Journal of Ethnic and Migration Studies, Comparative Education Review, Social Indicators Research, British Educational Research Journal, British Journal of Educational Studies, International Journal of Comparative Sociology,* and *Compare, a Journal of Comparative and International Education*. His latest book is *Regimes of Social Cohesion: Societies and the crisis of globalization*. He is also the main editor of *The Dynamics and Social Outcomes of Education Systems*. He was awarded a two-year Marie Curie Intra-European Fellowship for a proposal on education and identity-construction in post-communist states. He received a British Academy Mid-Career Fellowship for a research project on the value-added effect of school social and ethnic composition on civic attitudes. He contributed to bids for the ESRC-funded LLAKES Research Centre. He is currently leader of one of its themes, which explores the socio-cultural effects of lifelong learning systems through international comparative analysis.

Introduction

The context of learning

Why this book?

The dominant debate in British government points to perceived failures around multiculturalism and good community relations in the UK. Recent discourses surrounding faith schools, in particular, have focused on the failure of policies supporting multiculturalism to deliver community cohesion and tolerance in a democratic society. Faith schools are an entrenched part of UK society, and the agenda for parental choice suggests a continual expansion of these schools grounded in a religious ethos. By examining how parents and faith schools are engaging in the wider community, we can better determine how they can prepare their children for the challenges of the twenty-first century. The jury is out on the vision and success of multiculturalism in Britain. It is clear that the space between assimilation and integration is contested and very personal, and is therefore difficult to build into the wider public policy.

This book explores the important role that community engagement can play in faith schools as they create environments supportive of twenty-first-century learning. It is important to state that in this publication we are not advocating or denigrating faith schools and we do not view them as a threat to multiculturalism per se. Rather, what we aim to convey is:

- the experiences of some Jewish and Muslim schools within England;
- a more detailed understanding of Jewish and Muslim concepts of community;
- alternatives for preparing children for the skills and knowledge needed in the twenty-first century; and
- the implications for policy and practice in faith schools and those not characterized by a religious ethos or affiliation.

Jewish and Muslim schools have particularly faced public scrutiny in Britain, and though they constitute two very different types of communities they share, among other things, an experience of attracting intolerance and criticism, often in the form of anti-Semitism and Islamophobia. This book helps fill the gap in our understanding of these particular faith schools, exploring the role they play in sustaining their own religious heritage while also engaging with the wider society. We selected these faiths in part because of a dearth of content in the literature and also because they are well established and representative of visually discernible minority groups. We do not seek to compare or contrast one type of faith school with the other, but rather we look to how each type of faith school operates with respect to community engagement within the wider landscape of faith schools, drawing on our case study data.

Overview of the case study

It is important in this chapter to introduce our case study research which informs discussion throughout the book. Through an ESRC-funded project (Parker-Jenkins, 2008; Parker-Jenkins and Glenn, 2011), we explored the tension between different schools promoting a distinct identity. The main aims of the research were to explore why, and in what ways, religious/cultural sustainability is regarded as critical to the school's *raison d'être*, and what the experiences of engagement and estrangement or alienation with the wider community were. This research was built on the previous work of Parker-Jenkins, Hartas, and Irving (2005), which raised the question, 'do we ask enough of faith-based schools in terms of community engagement on behalf of their pupils?'. Access to a range of schools based on a Jewish or Islamic religious ethos was negotiated through senior members of these communities (Hammersley and Atkinson, 2007). These schools were selected for the case study with guidance from the Association of Muslim Schools-UK, the Leo Baeck College Centre for Jewish Education, and the United Synagogue Agency for Jewish Education.

We must state at the outset that there is huge diversity within Muslim schools in England based on sectarian, ethnic, linguistic, generational, and socio-economic distinctions among Muslim communities. They include mosque schools, supplementary schools, *madrassahs*, community schools with a majority of Muslim pupils, *Darul Uloom* schools, seminaries, boarding schools, institutions affiliated to the Association of Muslim Schools (AMS UK), and private/independent and state-funded/voluntary aided (VA) schools. So the word 'Muslim school' is an umbrella term including a wide range of schools with different understandings of Islamic principles and community engagement. Likewise, the term 'Jewish school' covers a variety of institutions presenting different teachings of Judaism and diverse levels of engagement with the external community. This differential within both categories of schools is discussed later in Chapters 3 and 4.

The fieldwork took place during 2007–08 and involved a case study of nine schools in the Midlands, London, the Home Counties, and Northern

The context of learning

England, with over 100 stakeholder participants. Senior managers, governors, teachers, parents, pupil/student focus groups, and members of the wider communities, such as imams and rabbis, provided data to relate to wider issues (Wellington, 2000). The study involved various data-gathering aspects, which both used theory and also contributed to its development and application (Berg, 2011). While 'voluntary aided' rather than 'voluntary controlled' status provides faith schools with greater levels of autonomy (Francis and Lankshear, 2001), the further inclusion of independent Jewish and Muslim schools in the case study enriched the exploration of 'self-exclusion' (Denham, 2001) reflected in different levels of social engagement.

Within the study we explored how Jewish and Muslim school communities seek to maintain internal community coherence, protect against threats of identity erosion, and protect against anti-Semitism and Islamophobia through influence over the education of their children in faith schools in England. We were particularly interested in how anti-Semitic and Islamophobic hostility surfaced toward schools formed by Jewish and Muslim communities and how this bodes in terms of engagement with the wider community. The case study involved analysing the experiences and challenges of the school community, which is made up of children, parents, teachers, and representatives of the wider community. Choices made regarding the curriculum, after-school activities, school ethos, school leadership, and community engagement were also included in the study.

The case study provides an insight into how these educational institutions, established with different religious underpinnings, provide a tailored design to meet their own contextual needs and challenges. One-to-one interviews and focus groups were chosen as the main research methods because of their use of questions of a sensitive nature (Cohen *et al.*, 2000; 2008), particularly concerning personal identity (Gunaratnam, 2003). The respondents' experiences were seen as partly constructed and shaped through the context of the school and the wider community through the process of reflexivity. Our approach endeavoured to understand the experiences and challenges of the children, parents, teachers, and representatives of the community, and the choices they make in their everyday lives. The study incorporated semi-structured interviews with stakeholders in each school, and discussion groups with pupils aged 8–18 through School Council selection or with older pupils. The data were subjected to thematic analysis using NVivo software (Denzin and Lincoln, 2002) to aid in the categorizing of themes such as community engagement and experiences of hostility. From this, we proposed a theoretical model as a framework, identifying different levels of engagement and providing a tool with which faith schools can evaluate achievements to date and identify possible future directions.

We focused specifically on full-time, faith-based education at primary and secondary level (that is, compulsory schooling for 15–16-year olds) in independent and state-funded VA schools (Francis and Lankshear, 2001). The education provided by these schools was distinct from classes delivered through supplementary education in the form of *madrassahs*, which deliver theologically-driven Islamic education, or *yeshiva* schools of intense religious learning, which are usually favoured in orthodox Judaism. While some groups are prompted to engage across, and within, religious boundaries and to participate in wider civil society and processes of governance, others seek to distance themselves from other religious traditions and secular culture. To ensure a wide spectrum, our research included liberal, progressive, pluralist and modern orthodox Jewish schools, and Muslim schools funded by the government or independent orthodox institutions. This formed a key area of inquiry in our research. Offering full-time education, the selected schools had greater opportunity to develop education thanks to extra or enhanced resource availability and strong pedagogical development by engagement with regulatory frameworks, quality assurance bodies, and mechanisms.

In short, the study involved a case study approach (Yin, 2009; Merriam, 2009) examining four Jewish schools and five Muslim schools representative of primary/elementary and secondary/high school levels, and incorporated institutions ranging from independent to state-funded within both religious traditions. The slight discrepancy in numbers was based on a decision to include a Muslim girls' school headed by a non-Muslim headteacher, which allowed us to provide the widest spectrum of perspectives. Children in the Jewish schools were mostly from families established in the UK for many decades and generally representative of European backgrounds. Those in the Muslim schools were predominantly second or third-generation British Muslims from diverse backgrounds, for example Pakistani, Bangladeshi, and Middle Eastern. Recent empirical studies on second- and third-generation British South Asians have noted an increasing tendency among British Pakistanis and Bangladeshis to assert their Muslim identities (Shain, 2011).

Scholars have focused on the complexity of the concepts of anti-Semitism and Islamophobia. Our working definition of the former was 'a certain perception of Jews, which may be expressed as hatred toward Jews' (European Monitoring Centre on Racism and Xenophobia, 2009: 1). Similarly, we defined Islamophobia as 'the unfounded hostility toward Islam, and fear or dislike of all or most Muslims' (Runnymede Trust, 2007:

The context of learning

1). We used Denham's (2001) concept of self-segregation by choice as it relates to cultural sustainability within schools. For the purpose of this discussion, we defined cultural sustainability as the passing on of traditions, customs, and values through the family or community, and the extent to which it is possible for Jews and Muslims to operate in a non-Jewish or non-Islamic society.

Organization of the book

In organizing the book, we first provide the overall objectives of the publication followed by brief discussion of key concepts here in the Introduction. Chapter 1 offers a historical perspective on faith schools, their origins in England and Wales based on Christian and Jewish traditions, and the expansion of the educational landscape to include other faith groups such as those based on an Islamic ethos. The historical patterns of accommodation between church and state are explored with brief reference to other European countries, drawing on examples from Scotland, Northern Ireland, and the Netherlands. Separation of church and state is discussed with reference to France and the development of a secular educational system. The evolution of Jewish and Muslim schools in the UK is also examined in preparation for the later chapters on the nature of these particular schools. Chapter 2 is concerned with faith schools and social policy, introducing the debates around diversity and cohesion in contemporary multicultural Britain. This is in the post-9/11 era, with rioting in northern cities in England (2001) and the 7/7 bombings in London (2005), which formed the context in which our case study took place. From this time, UK government policy has aimed to promote greater community cohesion in society. The role of schools has been seen as central to this initiative, and state-funded schools were required to provide evidence of having a role in promoting community cohesion (Home Office, 2004: 5). This chapter examines policy movement, from community cohesion under New Labour to the coalition government's notion of the 'Big Society'.

Chapters 3 and 4 examine the religious and cultural conceptions of community among the Jewish and Muslim faith groups and their differences based on ethnic, linguistic, and sectarian lines. Drawing on our case study research, we look at instances of hostility that schools have experienced and assess how these schools have coped with, and responded to, such incidents. We unearth experiences of hostility driven by anti-Semitism and Islamophobia (European Monitoring Centre on Racism and Xenophobia, 2009; Runnymede Trust, 2007), and examine how faith communities seek to keep themselves safe from the wider community. The findings of these chapters will then lead us, in Chapter 5, to promote *community engagement* as a more promising and productive perspective in assessing the relations of minority faith schools with the outside world, in comparison with the former policy of community cohesion. We look at what all schools can do to help develop better relations between groups in equipping children with twenty-first-century skills, building on our own model of community engagement rather than on community cohesion, and we examine practical curricula suggestions that all schools can adopt to develop tolerance and engagement with other groups. This leads to the final chapter of the book where we provide an overview of the discussion. Finally, looking forward, we suggest what the government should be doing, in light of the alleged 'failure of multiculturalism' (Kudani, 2002: 67), to address how faith schools fit within broader society.

Having provided an introduction to the central aims and organization of the book, we now introduce the key terminology and debates that are relevant to the overall discussion.

Key debates on faith schools

Central questions that we debate, in the context of faith schools, include the following:

- How can or do faith schools contribute to community engagement?
- How do internally strong communities cohere around certain ideas?
- What barriers or challenges do faith schools face in this regard?
- How do Jewish and Muslim faith schools successfully prepare young people for living and leading in a diverse world?

Multiculturalism in Britain and the role of faith schools

Sacks (2007) posits the theory that multiculturalism emerged as a reality based on large-scale migration toward Western countries from non-Western countries, which in turn led to the idea of 'one nation, one culture' (Sacks, 2007: 35). Immigration and the arrival of new communities to the UK have long been part of the discourse on multiculturalism and government policy. A key principle in multiculturalism has been respect for cultural difference, and that ethnic and religious minorities will only give their consent to be governed by the political institutions of the wider society when they are appreciated and promoted by the state (Lynch, 1987; Craft and Bardell, 1984; Berger, Galonska and Koopmans, 2004).

Supporters of faith schools argue that these educational institutions are well placed to contribute to the common good because they can provide children with a moral and religious framework that engenders confidence in their own identity and helps them to be respectful of the beliefs and values of others (Halstead and McLaughlin, 2005). Conversely, critics claim these schools make little effort to integrate, instead promoting intolerance and fundamentalist ideologies, and are detrimental to a harmonious society (Berkeley and Sevita, 2008; Dawkins, 2001).

There has been a shift from the concept of multiculturalism to one of community cohesion (Cantle, 2006) as an ideology within the liberal state (MacMullen, 2007). The failure of multiculturalism to deliver equitable outcomes in society and an attempt to look beyond this concept are echoed elsewhere, for example, by Hollinger (1995) and Kincheloe and Steinberg's (1997) work on critical multiculturalism. More recently, there have been political statements in France, Germany, and the UK that 'multiculturalism has failed' (Kudani, 2002: 67). The emphasis on 'bonding social capital' (Coleman, 1994; Pugh and Telhaj, 2007) assists in promoting shared values within the school community and a cooperative practice between the school and the home. The depth of social capital built within, and extending beyond, faith schools is a matter of degree – a point we aim to highlight throughout this book.

Religious identity and cultural diversity

There is often confusion over questions of religious identity and where race and religion merge or overlap. In other words, what part of a person's cultural identity and educational needs is based on their race or ethnic background, and which aspects concern their religious convictions? The term 'race' is used to describe genetic heritage (including skin colour and associated traits), while 'ethnicity' describes cultural background or allegiance (Taylor et al., 2002).

'Ethnicity' relates to a person's place of birth, symbolized by visible signifiers such as colour, dress, and lifestyle or birthplace allegiance (Barth, 1969; Hall, 1992; Modood and Werbner, 1997). 'Culture' is a complex expression of a sense of belonging and the passing on of customs and traditions (Giddens, 1995; Parekh, 2000; Werbner, 2002). Associated with this, the concept of 'identity' draws on a number of factors such as gender, age, and social class. It relates to the understandings people hold about who they are and what is meaningful to them. This involves self-designation and designation by others and can be constructed in terms of *either* or *all* of *religion*, *race*, or *ethnicity* (Giddens, 2001; Hall, 1992; Barth, 1969). This leads to a key question for educationalists: where does religion end and culture begin? Or, is it the other way round? Within an Islamic perspective, religious identity often takes primacy and is connected to social inclusion. For many, 'national identity is a technicality, a passport; and what matters is being part of the wider community or *ummah*' (Hulmes, 1989: 32). From a Jewish perspective, central to identity is the active commitment to maintain the activities of the Jewish faith (Miller, 2011; Sacks, 2007).

Enrolling children from diverse backgrounds is seen to increase engagement with wider social issues and enable young people to better understand different cultures and circumstances. However, this is a very fixed idea of what diversity is. Within Judaism and Islam there is a huge range of religious observance and ethnic backgrounds, and this needs to be reflected in how we view faith schools. One of the Muslim schools in our case study had pupils from six different ethnicities using ten different languages. Furthermore, 50 per cent of the staff were not Muslim. At one Jewish school in London that enrols pupils from outside of the Jewish faith, it was in fact a child from an Asian background who won the annual prize for Hebrew.

Education is an agency for cultural reproduction in both the public and private domains, and our study focused on minority communities that do not fit easily or neatly into the dominant national discourses (Parker-Jenkins, 1995; 2002). This book raises philosophical concerns relevant to government policy-formation and the alleged failure of multiculturalism (Kudani, 2002). Further, the book challenges the assumption that Jewish and Muslim schools withdraw or self-segregate from the wider community, and illustrates the ways that they engage and conceptualize local and wider communities and experience social engagement.

Parental choice in the UK

Since the 1950s, education policies in the UK have purposefully encouraged parental choice with a view to improving a bureaucratic and uniform education system. The practice of parental choice – particularly developed in the 1980s – has been a key concept that underpins the view that access to schooling is a basic right and duty reflected in parents' freedom to determine a child's educational path based on considerations of faith, academic success, and proximity to home. The Education Reform Act of 1988 introduced a school choice system that gave parents the right to express a preference for the school their child would attend (Burgess *et al.*, 2009). This was a significant ideological move from the neighbourhood-based system that was previously in place. The transition from a system in which pupils simply attended their local school to one in which parents were allowed to choose a school was intrinsically linked to school competition. The underlying notion

The context of learning

of these reforms was that more parental choice 'would increase education standards [and that] schools would improve their performance when they were forced to attract pupils' (ibid.: 3). The economic motivations for this shift were twofold. The first relates to allocation. Parents value different things in schools and more choice allows a better matching of pupils to schools based on both personal tastes and pedagogical needs. Competition through the mechanism of market discipline provided the other motivation. Parental choice was seen to be an effective way of ensuring that schools would offer high standards (Gibbons *et al.*, 2008).

Increased parental choice is itself contentious, with some claiming that the choice model privileges the middle classes (Webber and Butler, 2005; Taylor, 2006). Within the policy context, the Education and Inspections Act (2006) helped reinforce the emphasis on individualism, and political parties along the spectrum hesitate to challenge this view (Gorard *et al.*, 2003). The 'problem of choice' (Weekes-Bernard, 2007: i) is that it also leads to the segregation of children on the basis of religion, which, critics say, undermines attempts to create a more harmonious or tolerant society.

The theme of choice based on religious belief permeates this book. The significance of parental choice is reflected in human rights law. For example, the European Convention on Human Rights, to which the UK is a party, states that, in matters of education, countries must respect the religious or philosophical convictions of parents (Council of Europe, 1947: Protocol 1, Article 2). Dronkers *et al.* (2010) examined 24 countries and found that parental choice on behalf of children led to the emergence of two key patterns: the upper middle classes opting for private education, and the middle and lower-middle classes exercising choice which led to segregation. From a UK perspective, political parties across the spectrum have signalled support for choice in education, and this becomes more contentious when selection is based on religious considerations. Also, the commitment by the Labour government to expand faith schools in 1998 helped increase the numbers of educational institutions for children based on a range of religious traditions (DfE, 2012b). Both Jewish and Muslim schools have benefitted from this climate of support and, despite criticisms that the separation of children based on religious identity is divisive (Berkeley and Sevita, 2008), there is no indication that parental choice in this matter will be restricted. As we will see in this book, Jewish and Muslim school communities have developed an ethos that helps reflect shared religious values and supports compatibility between school and the home.

Competitive education strategies allow access to new social positions and can limit competition from members of the working classes (Dronkers *et al.*, 2010). Within the UK, most faith schools form part of public sector education, in terms of funding, resources, and support for professional development, among other areas. However, the state can still exercise control over private sector institutions, through curriculum standards, leadership, teaching requirements, and Ofsted inspections, despite the fact they receive no public funding (ibid.). Dronkers *et al.* (2010) argue that, in fact, parental choice is a direct result of changing economic and social spheres in the middle classes. Despite projects such as 'Accept Pluralism', an EU-funded project which sees some religious schools as part of the challenge to diversity and tolerance, there is a strong push for greater understanding across EU countries toward knowledge and skills within religious communities (Triandafyllidou, 2011).

There is a further risk that parents may change their lifestyle in order to manipulate their school choices. For example, parents may move house to improve the likelihood of gaining entry to their desired school or they may invest more time in religious activity to secure a place at a faith school. More importantly, there is no evidence so far that reveals that school competition through parental choice leads to any improvements in educational standards (Gibbons *et al.*, 2008).

Under the former Labour Government, faith schools were seen to be a vehicle for increased parental choice. Parents have been given the right in a modern society to choose whether they educate their child in a faith-based or secular school. The consideration that parents may choose schools that have a pupil intake with similar characteristics is particularly pertinent to faith schools. Burgess *et al.* (2009) found religion to be a significant factor for parents in choosing a school. Over 10 per cent stated religion to be an important factor in their first-choice nomination of a school. Gibbons *et al.* (2008) found that proximity to the family home was not a significant determinant for parents in choosing to send their child to a faith school. In fact, the highest rate of attendance in a different LEA from their own is from pupils in VA schools of which a significant majority are faith schools (Gibbons *et al.*, 2008).

There is little conclusive research on the reasons parents within the Jewish and Muslim faiths choose to send their children to a faith school. It is easy to speculate that this decision may be based on a desire for cultural sustainability, fear of assimilation, or religious continuity. For many Muslim parents faith is an integral part of their identity and they want faith to be an integral part of their child's education (Runnymede Trust, 2007). What we do know is that more parents are deciding to send their children to faith schools. According to the Jewish Leadership Council's (JLC's) 2011 report, *The Future of Jewish Schools*, 60 per cent of Jewish schoolchildren attended Jewish schools, compared with 50 per cent four years previously. This figure can be attributed to the increase in the strictly Orthodox Jewish community, with the figure for the mainstream Jewish community likely to be nearer 45 to 50 per cent. Parental demand for faith schools has also resulted in additional places being provided in these institutions. Further, since 2008, seven new state-aided faith schools and two independent ones have opened (DfE, n.d.). From a Muslim perspective, an Islamic ethos, single-sex schooling, high academic standards, and a safe haven from racism have been found to be significant in parental choice (Hewer, 2001; Parker-Jenkins, 2002).

A key claim by faith schools is that education is central to living as a Jew or a Muslim (for example) in the UK and beyond. Tailored educational learning is central to religious identity and practice and, we would argue, to the suite of twenty-first-century skills that will best prepare students for the future. Communities actively perpetuate and socialize according to faith-based values and traditions. Thus, importantly, we do not claim faith schools exist to defend against external pressure, but rather to help preserve cultural identity and enhance the skills that help prepare children to navigate life and lead.

Faith schools

The clergy was instrumental in initiating schooling based on denominational lines, hence the descriptor 'denominational schools'. Under legislative changes in the UK brought about by the Elementary Education Act (1870), it was recognized that religious groups could not afford to meet the educational needs of the country, and VA or voluntary aided schools were given financial assistance from the government, based along Anglican, Catholic, and Jewish lines (Francis and Lankshear, 2001). Similarly, this terminology was used in the Education Act (1944) and confirmed in the Education Reform Act (1988). Up until the twenty-first century, the terms 'voluntary' or 'church school' have been used interchangeably, but they are not synonymous: there are a few voluntary schools that are not premised on religious foundations, and there have been some VA Jewish schools since the nineteenth century (Miller, 2001).

The use of the term 'faith schools' has gained currency since the publication of the report *Schools: Building on success* (DfEE, 2001) which declared its support for 'the number and variety of schools within the state system supported by the churches and *other major faith groups*' (ibid.: 48, emphasis added). In terms of the shifting nomenclature used for religious schools, no single term adequately conveys the range of schools now being encouraged to develop, but for the purpose of our discussion we are using the term 'faith school' to include all those educational institutions that aspire to inculcate religious beliefs in children and to perpetuate a particular lifestyle.

Reviewing community cohesion

For this book we have used the definition of community cohesion provided in *Guidance on the Duty to Promote Community Cohesion* (DCSF, 2007a). In the UK, schools played an important role in promoting the now-defunct community cohesion policy for which we supply an alternative approach. The ways in which community cohesion has been understood, and has played out in policy and practice, are largely based on historical events and political perspectives. The political context that shaped the British Government's agenda on social cohesion included the 7/7 bombings in London and the riots in Northern towns in England in 2001 (Independent Review Team, 2001; HMSO, 2006). Trust was broken in many communities and issues about diversity and opportunity in a complex multi-racial society came to the fore.

Up until 2008, schools had a distinctive role in promoting the community cohesion agenda. The national goal was to ensure that 'all pupils understand and appreciate others from different backgrounds with a sense of shared values, fulfilling their potential and feeling part of a community, at a local, national, and international level' (ibid.: 2). Schools were encouraged to build community cohesion 'by promoting equality of opportunity and inclusion for different groups of pupils within a school and promoting shared values' (ibid.: 6). In practical terms, this was to be achieved through teaching and learning, working to raise standards and encourage a given ethos, and engaging with the community and extended (that is, wider public) services.

Within the lofty aspirations of community cohesion, a school's contribution to society was seen to be through the community and its extended services. These broad themes were particularly relevant to faith schools, since schools were seen as a venue for young people to interact with people from different backgrounds (DCSF, 2007a). All schools in the UK were obliged to foster community cohesion, but there was a particular emphasis on faith schools to implement the government initiative. They were singled out for criticism as a result of their self-imposed segregation: 'commitment to the promotion of cohesion is not universal, and for many faith schools, not a priority' (Berkeley and Sevita, 2008: 5).

The concept of cohesion in this simplistic form is particularly complicated for faith communities. As suggested in this critique of the policy, it was unclear what should be cohered around and whose values should underpin cohesion (Parker-Jenkins and Glenn, 2011). What were the deliverables and how might they be recognized? The various definitions of community imply that cohesion does not simply mean cohering within a community, but politically it implies reaching beyond the immediate community (Parker-Jenkins *et al.*, 2005). What has emerged is disillusionment with, and fear of, the ideologies of integration and assimilation.

The UK's policy of community cohesion has been abandoned since 2008, and now school communities are understandably confused as to what they should be doing in the absence of a clear governmental steer. Confusion over the Big Society initiative, which has been launched and re-launched, adds to the lack of credibility of this replacement policy.

Community engagement

We suggest the concept of *community engagement* as an alternative and more realistic approach to the now-abandoned policy of community cohesion. According to Pearce (2005), community engagement means promoting greater respect, knowledge, and contact between groups within the community, and fostering a stronger sense of citizenship. Measuring the variables of an agreed definition of cohesion is challenging. Community engagement is defined as the ability or willingness of different communities to live alongside and with each other, and to meet, work, and be educated with those outside of their own community (Gaine, 1995). As with community cohesion, associated with these concepts is that of alienation – meaning withdrawal, self-imposed segregation in the name of maintaining identity, or fear of others – thus to separate or disengage (Beckerman and McGlynn, 2007). For many minority ethnic groups (Dadzi, 2001), the promotion of assimilation, where names are anglicized and the only status that matters is framed around a white Christian perspective, is rejected. This is one of the reasons that faith schools emerged in the first place – disillusionment with, and fear of, the ideologies of integration and assimilation (Parker-Jenkins *et al.*, 2005).

There needs to be a holistic approach to securing community cohesion and family wellbeing, involving all service providers working together. With respect to community engagement, a comprehensive literature review provides effective strategies for schools to support and engage with families (Statham *et al.*, 2010). *The Children's Plan* notes that schools are 'well placed to become a focal point for the local community and to foster better relationships between diverse communities' (DCSF, 2007b: 73). The removal now of the legal obligation for schools to demonstrate what they have been doing to promote community cohesion, as highlighted earlier, may be viewed by some schools as one activity less that they have to contend with in the light of other government requirements, or as an opportunity to look at alternative approaches to preparing children for living in a multicultural society. We propose the term 'community engagement' in this book, arguing that it is a more helpful term than 'community cohesion', which is the language of aspiration and rhetoric.

The 'Big Society'

The UK Conservative–Liberal-Democrat coalition government which gained power in 2010 did not formally revoke the community cohesion policy but 'signalled its preference for achieving the integration of British ethnic minority communities through the Big Society narrative rather than that of community cohesion' (Rowe et al., 2011: 4). The Big Society initiative in the UK places an emphasis on people and communities and moves away from the state, with notions of autonomy, strong civil society, and providing for oneself (Inside Government, 2013a). Contrary to the previous government, the Department for Education (DfE) assigns only a minimal role to the state in promoting integration and social cohesion (DfE, 2010b). However, what the coalition government shares with the community cohesion agenda is a commitment to common values and 'Britishness' and a rejection of permissive multiculturalism. This is contrary to the wishes of minority ethnic groups if it is perceived to undermine their sense of identity, community, and their ability to prepare their children for life in the future.

Twenty-first-century skills in practice

The impetus for twenty-first-century skills (which will be defined and explored in Chapter 5) largely falls on schools to develop a skills-based pedagogy to equip children for the future. Under Section 78 of the Education Act (2002), schools are seen as locales for the 'physical, mental, social, cultural and moral development' of young people. The debate over whether faith schools provide the adequate development which prepares young people for adulthood and gives them the ability to operate effectively in a multi-ethnic, multi-faith society is filled with both praise and concern. On one side, faith schools are praised for giving pupils a strong sense of personal worth and preparing them to be good citizens (Ofsted, 2009). As a result, religious schools are seen as creating an atmosphere that is conducive to learning. Moreover, schools with high social capital have a significant advantage, which explains the successes of many faith schools – they have a ready-made sense of community. Effective communities combine the capacity to bond with the ability to bridge (West-Burnham et al., 2007). Work experience and placements were just one example we found in our case study of how faith schools help pupils develop twenty-first-century skills and prepare them for adulthood.

There are concerns, however, that a narrow curriculum prevents young people from participating in a pluralistic society outside of their own family and community (Bald et al., 2010). Opponents of faith schools maintain that children are raised in a segregated community, unaware of others outside of their faith group, and that this can lead to intolerance (Berkeley and Sevita, 2008; Dawkins, 2001).

Although Berkeley and Sevita (2008) do contend that pupils in faith schools gain valuable communication and collaboration skills as a result of a value-based education and strong ties with the community, this, they suggest, is not enough to prepare young people for living and working in a multi-faith society, because of the limited opportunities for young people to mix with people of different backgrounds.

Performance and faith schools

Parental choice is influenced by a number of factors apart from religious ethos, one of which is the academic success of a school. The presence of religious state-funded secondary schools in England impacts the educational experiences of pupils who attend neighbouring schools, whether through school effort induced by competition or changes in peer groups induced by selection. National administrative data estimate pupil test score growth models between the ages of 11 and 16, with instrumental variable methods employed to avoid confounding the direct causal effect of religious schools. VA status gives faith schools majority representation on the governing body and therefore control over the employment of staff, buildings and repairs, and school admissions (Gay and Greenough, 2000). There appears to be significant evidence that religious schools are associated with higher levels of pupil selection across schools, but no evidence that competition from faith schools raises area-wide pupil attainment (Allen and Vignoles, 2010. Also see generally Gibbons et al. (2008); Yeshanew et al. (2008); Schagen and Schagen (2005); and Pettinger (2012). Little evidence in the literature exists, however, regarding the impact of school admission policies using the former community cohesion policy (Statham et al., 2010).

The Ofsted Framework for School Inspection

Since September 2012, Ofsted's *Framework for School Inspection* has focused on the features of a school's work that raise achievement levels. The Ofsted evaluation is not limited to academic achievement but includes broader aspects such as the 'spiritual, moral, social and cultural development' of pupils (Ofsted, 2013: 20). In achieving this goal, Ofsted determines that schools must provide an inclusive environment for all pupils, irrespective of religion or belief, which is free from bullying, harassment, and discrimination (ibid.).

Further, according to this government agency, the school curriculum must reflect these goals and:

> provide a broad and balanced curriculum that meets the needs of all pupils, enables all pupils to achieve their full educational potential and make progress in their learning, and promotes their good behaviour and safety.
>
> (Ofsted, 2013: 20)

According to Ofsted, a 'good' or 'outstanding' school is deemed to be one in which the leadership or management of the school engages parents in supporting their children's achievements and their 'spiritual, moral, social and cultural development' (ibid.).

Having provided an introduction to the central aims and organization of the book and the key terminology and debates, we look next at the historical and legal background to faith schools and how the tradition of establishing schools based on a religious ethos began in England and Wales, and elsewhere.

Chapter 1
Faith schools
Historical and legal background

Individuals may belong to a number of communities during their lifetime. These include communities of family or kinship, or school or religious belief. For some people, two communities overlap in the form of religion and the choice of school, and decisions concerning membership in these groups are informed by the way they construct their lives. The relationship between church and state has been instrumental in the historical development of public education in England and Wales. Schooling based on Anglican, Catholic, and Jewish teaching has been supported in the UK for some time. In this chapter, we provide a historical and legal perspective on religious schooling in England and Wales, highlighting the role of the clergy in establishing academic institutions based on Christian lines, and the use of government funds to support their development. This provides a framework for understanding the guiding principles behind present policies relating to religious education. Furthermore, this chapter explores the extent to which present concerns about faith schools as a possible threat to social cohesion and/or community engagement are not new in political discourses. Finally, a variety of national contexts are also examined to help demonstrate how other countries have responded to religious pluralism and schooling.

The discussion begins with an examination of the origins of mass education and the role of the church in England and Wales in initiating formal education for all children. We then address:

- the evolution of Jewish and Muslim schools in England and Wales;
- faith schools in Scotland, Northern Ireland, and the Netherlands;
- and the secular tradition in France.

Denominational schooling in England and Wales
Educational provision in England and Wales established on denominational lines dates back to the Middle Ages, and faith-based groups have continued to preserve this tradition. By the nineteenth century, major social and economic upheaval due to the direct consequences of the Industrial Revolution called for social policy enactment. Education was considered an important agent of social reform to assist the nation in its economic

endeavours. Government at this time was, however, somewhat ambivalent about its role in the provision of educational services. Furthermore, the Victorians were said to be suspicious of government involvement in daily events and feared the growth of state intervention into what had, hitherto, been a purely private concern (Curtis and Boultwood, 1966).

Prior to 1850, what provision there was for educating the 'poorer classes' – that is, people legislatively classified as those who supported themselves by manual labour (see Wardle, 1976: 117) – was by virtue of the charity schools founded by such organizations as the British and Foreign School Society of 1810 and National Schools, established in 1811. Throughout England and Wales, the clergy initiated schooling as a means of carving out their evangelical mission. While government began subsidizing education to a limited degree in the form of treasury grants in 1833, it did not assume the role of instigator for educational provision, and universal free schooling was not implemented until the following century (Armitage, 1964). Instead, faith groups were instrumental in promoting education with a strong inculcation of religious values (Wolffe, 1994) and they began a tradition of denominational schooling that has continued to the present day. Furthermore, when the state did choose to venture into providing education for all children, the clergy continued to have influence; indeed, education and Christianity were inextricably linked in the public mind (Tropp, 1957).

The Catholic Church was also instrumental in establishing schools in England and Wales. Emancipation in the 1830s gave Catholics the possibility of establishing their own schools and obtaining state funding (Grace, 2001). A major purpose of the Catholic Church in voluntarily establishing schools was to introduce children to matters of faith via the curriculum. Staffing policy was considered of major importance in this respect, accompanied by a desire to have freedom from government interference (Hickman, 1995; O'Keefe, 2000; Church Schools Review Group, 2001; Catholic Education Service [CES], 2003). This forms part of the ongoing challenge facing Catholic schools today, which, like Church of England schools, are still having to redefine themselves and their mission within and beyond the school community (CES, 1998, 1999, 2000; Conroy and McCreath, 1999; Eaton et al., 2000). In addition to adapting to accommodate non-Catholics, Catholic schools are also perceived as providing high academic attainment, in keeping with other faith schools. In England, there are over 2,000 Catholic schools, which stand alongside Church of England schools as a central feature of faith-based schooling, accommodating approximately 10 per cent of children of school age (CES 2012, section 8).

By the 1860s, it was clear that faith-based groups voluntarily establishing schools alone could not adequately meet the needs of the nation. At the time, arguments were presented for both the expansion of church schools and the creation of a wholly secular system. The Elementary School Act (1870), which established a primary school system for all, was seen as a compromise in that voluntary schools were allowed to continue with state funding. This was augmented by the establishment of state schools run by local school boards (Lankshear, 1996; Lankshear and Hall, 2003). Christianity was still taught, but schools were forbidden to promote one denomination over another, and parents had the right to withdraw their children from religious instruction. At the end of the nineteenth century, the voluntary sector had established around 14,000 schools representative of religious groups, including the Church of England, Catholic, Methodist, and Wesleyan groups (Archbishop's Council Church Schools Review Group, 2001: 6). Further, categories of denominational schools were designated in the Education Act (1944) with various levels of government control, but generally referred to as 'voluntary' schools (Arthur, 1995; Francis and Lankshear, 2001). Schools were offered the option of either increased funding and control, hence 'voluntary controlled schools', which became common practice among Church of England schools (Arthur, 1995; Lankshear, 2003), or less support and state interference, together with greater independence, known as 'voluntary aided', a status assumed by the majority of Catholic schools (Grace, 2001; O'Keefe, 1999, 2000).

The legal context

The 1944 Act did not specify religious affiliation. The relevant clauses of the Act provided for different levels of support and state intervention, but they did not specify *which* denominational groups could be included in the scheme. Hence, Jewish schools have received state funding through the procedure of obtaining VA status (Miller, 2001), and more recently so have Muslim, Sikh, Greek Orthodox, and Seventh Day Adventist schools (Gov.uk, 2014; CES, 2012; Bolton and Gillie, 2009: 3). Other minority groups may also wish to avail themselves of this right in the future, which is consistent with government thinking on the matter. As faith-based communities have initiated schooling and expanded provision, their role has been increasingly underpinned by legislation, which has helped reinforce their place in helping to establish a national system of education in England and Wales, beginning in the nineteenth century, and continuing up until the present (Cush, 2003).

Between 1986 and 2002, there were 16 Education Acts in England and Wales, and the partnership between church and state continued to develop through various reforms and changes (National Society, 2003). The School Standards and Framework Act (1998) is particularly noteworthy because it contains a number of provisions that bring faith-based school communities substantially into the decision-making process.

The Act created four categories of schools within the state system in England and Wales, namely:

- community schools (formerly County schools);
- foundation schools (formerly Grant Maintained schools);
- VA schools;
- and voluntary controlled schools.

All community schools must implement the locally 'Agreed Syllabus' as a basis for religious education and must not have a religious character (Jackson, 2003). Schools within the other categories may have a religious character based on the school's trust deed or traditional practice. All schools that have a religious character may have a collective act of worship reflective of the religious group concerned, but only those designated as having VA status may have denominational religious education. This legislation also aims to make decisions a matter for collective agreement at both national and local levels and for the church or other groups to work in partnership with government.

A number of statutes concerning faith schools are directly relevant to the expansion of this category of school. The Education Act (1996) has relevance for all independent schools and is an important piece of legislation in that new faith schools have tended to become independent first and then subsequently apply for state funding. This is what has happened in the case of Muslim and Sikh schools, for example, and is an approach likely to be followed by other minority groups (Parker-Jenkins *et al.*, 2005).

This is within the context of competing discourses about the wisdom of having faith schools (Dawkins, 2001; British Humanist Association, 2002) set against the valuing of having alternative sites for learning and religious expression (Grace, 2003; Pring, 2005; Short, 2002) which we highlighted in the Introduction. Halstead and McLaughlin (2005) state:

> … children who have a strong self-identity and who are treated fairly and justly by the broader society are much more likely to grow up into tolerant, balanced and responsible citizens.
>
> (Halstead and McLaughlin, 2005: 67)

The Education Act (1996) defines a school as one in which there are more than five pupils of compulsory school age, and as such a school can even be – and has been – established in a person's sitting room. Fewer than five pupils and the arrangement is seen as constituting the 'education otherwise' category as stipulated in the Education Act (1944), that is, education taking place at home on an individual or small-group basis rather than at a school. If there are more than five children, then an application is made to the Department for Education and Skills (DfES) to be registered as an independent school. In order to do this, the institution has to comply under a number of headings. These relate to the suitability of the premises, accommodation regarding the age of the pupils, and facilities if boarding children. 'Suitable and efficient' teaching and learning are also required, and the curriculum should be generally broad and balanced. Independent schools do not have to teach all of the National Curriculum, nor do they have to employ qualified teachers. There is a body of regulations with which independent schools are required to comply that contrasts with the public image of them being totally unregulated institutions (see, for example, ISC, 2014). It is not the remit of this chapter to address the specifics of the curricular requirements of faith schools; rather, we address these in more general terms in Chapters 3 and 4 with reference to Jewish and Muslim schools.

In terms of inspection and accountability, state-funded faith schools are inspected just like all other maintained schools except in terms of religious education. The social, cultural, spiritual, and moral aspects of the school are covered under Section 23 of the 1996 Act. After September 2003, reports on independent schools were to be placed in the public domain and made available on the Ofsted website (Ofsted, 2013). The framework provides that these reports be specific with regard to premises, welfare, and arrangements for the school having a complaints procedure. Also relevant in discussing the legal context of faith schools is the School Standards and Framework Act (1998). This provided for the creation of School Organization Committees consisting of representatives of the Local Education Authority, governing bodies, and the Learning and Skills Council. In the absence of an agreement over an issue, an adjudicator appointed by the Secretary of State would take a decision.

In considering candidates for the position of headteacher of a voluntary controlled or VA school, a governing body may, as Lankshear (2001) notes, take into consideration the candidate's ability to maintain and nurture the religious character of the school. This has been reiterated under the Independent Schools (Employment of Teachers in Schools with a Religious Character) Regulation (2003) as follows: preference may be given in connection with the appointment, promotion, or remuneration at a faith school of teachers 'whose religious opinions are in accordance with the tenets of the religion or the religious denomination specified in relation to the school' or 'who give, or who are willing to give, religious education at the school in accordance with those tenets' (section 124A). Likewise, the admissions policy for pupils is informed by religious considerations. We note here that the ability for wide-ranging religious considerations to be taken into account by a faith school in admissions was curtailed in 2009 by the Supreme Court ruling in the JFS case (R on application of E v Governing Body of JFS and the Admissions Appeal Panel of JFS [2009] UKSC 15), which is discussed in more detail in Chapter 3. We will also return to this point later in the chapter with reference to Catholic schools in Scotland.

The expansion of faith schools can also be seen as part of a government strategy to extend the provision of a category of schools that it sees as being successful in terms of parental support and academic attainment. At the beginning of this chapter, we looked at the early faith schools in England and Wales dating back to the seventeenth century and their relationship with the state in building a national system of education. The development of schooling has also been impacted by successive waves of immigrants to Britain. In the post-1950s era, there was significant immigration, this time from the Caribbean, Asia, and East Africa particularly, which has led to the establishment of several new faith communities. The new faith schools emerging from these communities have been established in the last 20 years and mainly serve the children of first- or second-generation immigrants. Some have succeeded in obtaining state support since 1998.

The educational landscape in England and Wales now includes faith schools from a variety of religious backgrounds. This book focuses on those established by Jewish and Muslim communities.

The establishment of Jewish and Muslim schools in England and Wales

The Jewish education system in England and Wales can be traced back to the mid-seventeenth century. Following the re-admittance of Jews into England in 1656 (Romain, 1985), Jewish day schools were established alongside synagogues, notably the Creechurch Lane Talmud Torah School in 1657 and the Gates of Hope School in 1664 (Black, 1998). As we saw earlier in this chapter, there was an urgent demand to meet the need for an educated workforce in the eighteenth and nineteenth centuries, and the establishment of Jewish schools such as the Jews' Free School in 1732 helped to respond to this call (ibid.).

Meanwhile, the history of Muslim schooling in the country has been associated with the struggle for parity with other faith schools, along

Faith schools

the lines of that afforded to Christian and Jewish institutions. As Hewer (2001) notes, there have been Muslims in Britain for centuries, but issues of accommodation within the educational system did not arise until the post-1950s immigration period. In addition, the obstacles Muslim communities have faced have been magnified because their supporters are predominantly representative of differing ethnic minorities, and this particular wave of immigration raises 'complex issues of colour, race and religion' (ibid.: 515).

The 2011 Census revealed that in terms of religious affiliation, there are just over 2.7 million Muslims in the UK and just under 280,000 Jews (Office of National Statistics, 2011). As a result of immigration there is diversity within the UK Jewish community, most notably Ashkenazi Jews (from Eastern Europe) and Sephardi Jews (from the Near East and the Iberian Peninsula), and major Jewish centres established in London and Manchester reflect the cultural differences (Schmool and Cohen, 1998). In terms of Jewish schools, there are 96 full-time Jewish educational institutions in the UK; 41 per cent of them are state-funded, serving approximately 30,000 children of compulsory school age (5–16) and representing 50 per cent of the Jewish pupil population (Miller, 2007: 2012). Today, there are over 100 Jewish schools in England and Wales, 43 of which operate full-time with government funding (DfE, n.d.). The categorization of Jewish schools is discussed in more detail in Chapter 3.

Both Jewish and Muslim school communities are following in the steps of previous denominational groups, notably Anglican (Brown, 2003; Francis and Lankshear, 2001) and Catholic (Hornsby-Smith, 2000; CES, 1997), in establishing schools permeated by faith. Muslim schools have tended to be the group targeted for greatest criticism in trying to follow this denominational school tradition, accessing the public purse, and in some cases allegedly teaching a 'radical' Islam and more divisive views (Parker-Jenkins, 2002). As we know from research on Catholic schools (O'Keefe, 1997; CES, 1999) and Jewish schools (JLC, 2010; Short and Lenga, 2002), there are different levels of engagement with the wider community by faith schools and their self-exclusion can be construed to demonstrate deliberate social isolation (O'Keefe, 1997), sometimes in the form of ethnic/religious defence (Husain and O'Brien, 1999). Both Jewish and Muslim schools achieve cultural sustainability through the medium of education, and both experience hostility unlike other faith groups in the form of anti-Semitism and Islamophobia (Runnymede Trust, 1994, 1997, 2007; Allen and Nielsen, 2002; Community Security Trust [CST], 2012).

Within Jewish schools, Pikuach – an inspection service launched by the Board of Deputies of British Jews in 1996 – is the UK Jewish community's response to the government's requirement that religious education be inspected under the framework set up by Ofsted. In recent years, Pikuach reports, or religious inspections, have emphasized the role that school self-evaluation plays as part of the examination process (Miller, 2007, 2011). Similarly, guidance can be sought from the Association of Muslim Schools on inspection services for those institutions based on an Islamic ethos (Association of Muslim Schools [AMS UK], n.d.).

Francis and Robbins (2011) state that three kinds of faith schools have emerged in England: state-maintained institutions, 'traditional' independent schools, and 'new' independent schools. The provision of faith education through state-maintained schools was secured under the Education Act (1944) as we saw earlier. Faith schools under the Education Act (1944) account for a third of state-maintained primary schools and a tenth of state-maintained secondary schools (Francis and Robbins, 2011). 'Traditional' and 'new' independent schools, alternatively, developed directly out of religious communities, founded by organizations and individual benefactors wishing to secure a religious ethos. A handful of Jewish schools claimed VA status at the time of the Education Act (1944), and more recently a number of schools from other faiths have been added to this category (Francis and Robbins, 2011; DfE, n.d.). Among the 'new' independent schools are those founded by Muslim communities, some of which are linked to AMS UK.

Statistically, Muslim schools have been the most rapidly expanding faith-based group. Twenty years ago there were approximately 25 Muslim schools in the UK, some beginning as small groups taught in parents' homes or above a mosque (Parker-Jenkins, 1995). As noted in the introductory chapter, there is huge diversity within Muslim schools in the UK based on sectarian, ethnic, linguistic, generational, and socio-economic distinctions among Muslim communities. They include mosque schools, supplementary schools, *madrassahs*, community schools with a majority of Muslim pupils, *Darul Uloom* schools, seminaries, boarding schools, institutions affiliated to AMS UK, and private/independent and state-funded/VA schools. So the word 'Muslim school' is an umbrella term including a wide range of schools with different understandings of Islamic principles and community engagement (we highlight this point later in Chapter 4).

Today there are approximately 160 schools in this religious grouping, and they are mostly Sunni, which reflects the fact that only 10 per cent of Muslim communities in Britain are Shia (AMS UK, n.d.). Of the Muslim population in the UK, approximately 350,000 are of school age (ibid.). In terms of institutions, Muslim schools form part of the educational landscape. There are approximately 7,000 state-funded, faith-based schools in England. These include just under 5,000 Church of England and other Christian schools; 2,053 Catholic schools; 43 Jewish schools; 11 Muslim schools; 4 Sikh schools; and one each of a Hindu, Seventh Day Adventist, Quaker, and Greek Orthodox school. Together, these faith-based schools represent a third of all state-funded schools (DfE, n.d.). The obligation to teach to the English National Curriculum (DfEE, 2001) falls on those schools in receipt of public funding, but many Jewish and Muslim schools incorporate aspects of the national framework into their curriculum (Parker-Jenkins and Glenn, 2011). Further, independent faith schools are required to teach a certain percentage of this curriculum as part of their registration with the DfE. Faith schools inspired by various understandings of Islamic principles have developed, since the immigration wave of the 1960s, due to a number of factors including increased dissatisfaction with community school provision (Walford, 2001; Hewer, 2001; Parker Jenkins, 2002). Notwithstanding geographical, historical, and cultural differences, the parallel growth of both Jewish and Muslim schools in the UK highlights fundamental issues of community engagement and religious identity.

Currently there is a wide range of faith schools receiving state funding, the majority of which are more correctly described as 'voluntary controlled' and VA, an important distinction we discussed earlier. There is also a variety of other types of schools, for example academies and foundation schools, that may or may not have religious sponsors, and the remaining community schools, which tend to be non-denominational (Education and Inspections Act, 2006). We should also make mention here of foundation schools and City Technology Colleges (CTCs); these are owned by trustees and may or may not have a religious ethos (Edwards *et al.*, 1993). There is understandable confusion over the status of some CTCs – the new academies that are state-funded but independent of local government control (Gov.uk, 2014) – where the sponsor is associated with a religious group. In these cases, the institutions are not normally deemed to be faith schools, yet their sponsorship and importantly the composition of their governing bodies may reflect a religious tradition.

So far in our discussions we have traced the historical development of faith schools, the proposal for their expansion, and the legal framework in which they operate. Supporters claim that it is not about privileging faith schools but creating opportunities for new providers of education, especially in disadvantaged areas where schools are seen to be failing, as we will further discuss in Chapter 2. Where there are existing independent faith schools, the government sees advantages in bringing them into the maintained sector.

Having provided a historical background to faith schools in England and Wales, discussion turns now to other national contexts, which will provide a useful comparison in order to understand faith school trends and the different degrees of school autonomy.

Faith schools in Scotland, Northern Ireland, and the Netherlands, and the secular tradition in France

Scotland

Education in Scotland has been influenced by religious traditions, in keeping with developments south of the border, predominantly those related to Protestantism and Catholicism. There are distinctions to be made between the Scottish variety of Catholic education and its counterparts in England and Wales and in Northern Ireland. The distinctive nature of this education system is, according to Conroy (2001), a consequence of three important and interrelated features of Scottish history. The first is the religious history of Scotland and its impact on the evolution of educational provision. Second, we have the particular patterns of migration that affected Scotland, especially from the end of the eighteenth century through to the early part of the twentieth century. Finally, the distinctive legal and legislative history of Scotland has been important in producing subtle differences in major Education Acts of the late nineteenth and twentieth centuries.

There are claims that Catholic schools in Scotland are no longer relevant since most of the children in attendance are no longer practicing Catholics (Conroy, 2001). Bruce *et al.* (2005) add to this debate, noting that allegiance to Catholic Christianity is allegedly dangerous to the good functioning of the state because it is divisive and anti-social. (The concerns, from Protestants, expressed in terms of Catholic education posing a threat to cohesion and the state, are the very same as ones being expressed today regarding Muslim faith schools.) Conversely, Conroy counters that in twenty-first-century Scotland, the health of a liberal society depends on the toleration and accommodation of difference. According to Conroy, the reason for antagonism against Catholics in Scotland is rooted in the continuing legacy of the bitter anti-Catholic sentiment evident in the country, which dates back to before the twentieth century. This, in part, is due to the belief that Catholic schools employ discriminatory employment practices. Proponents counter this by arguing that they seek to employ teachers who can contribute to developing the ethos on which the school is founded, in keeping with other faith-based groups. They also, according to Davis (1999), provide the possibility of alternative ways of constructing and making sense of the world. This resonates with arguments put forward for the establishment of other denominational schools in the UK in the twenty-first century, for example Muslim, Hindu, and Sikh institutions (Parker-Jenkins *et al.*, 2005). Furthermore, it should be noted that although there is one Jewish school and a small number of Episcopalian schools (McKinney, 2008), and there have been attempts to establish Muslim schools in Scotland due to parental demand (Herald Scotland, 2012), debates about the relevance of faith schooling remain predominantly focused on Catholic education, which provides the main form of state-funded, faith-based education in Scotland and which has traditionally experienced sustained criticism and suspicion.

Northern Ireland

Northern Ireland has a long history of conflict based on a struggle between those who wish to see it remain part of the UK (mainly Protestants) and those who may wish to have a united Ireland (predominantly Catholics). The majority of people still live in single-identity communities, either Protestant or Catholic, and 97 per cent of the Northern Irish population attends religion-specific schools (Church *et al.*, 2004; Gallagher, 1995).

When discussing faith schools, Northern Ireland is often singled out as a particular case to highlight the controversy associated with educating children in segregated institutions based on religious difference. General discussion about religion and education in liberal societies can be applied to Northern Ireland, but Wright (2003) suggests its particular political and cultural context demands that it be treated as a special case. Due to the intertwining of cultural, religious, and political identities in Northern Ireland, debates about the role of religion in education have been strongly influenced by local and historical factors.

Historically, a national system of education at primary school level developed in Ireland in the nineteenth century and, initially, a multi-denominational system was envisaged, but political unrest reflected the divergent interests of Protestants and Catholics with regard to their affiliation to the UK (Gallagher and Cairns, 2011; Cairns and Darby, 1995). A parallel religious school system eventually developed, reflecting the political mood of the time. While the separate school system continued, various intervention strategies were planned and the 1990s was a time of major government initiatives for promoting better community relations.

The essence of the debate concerns the right to separate education in a pluralist society, against the role that separate schools are perceived to play in perpetuating division and sectarianism (Grace, 2003; Short, 2003; Gallagher, 2004; Berkeley and Sevita, 2008). As we noted in the introductory chapter, supporters of faith schools argue that such schools are well placed to contribute to the common good because they can provide children with a moral and religious framework that engenders confidence in their own identity and helps them to be respectful of the beliefs and values of others (Halstead and McLaughlin, 2005).

In Northern Ireland, where over 92 per cent of Protestant and Catholic children are educated with co-religionists (Department of Education Northern Ireland, 2012), controversy over the role of a parallel education system in fostering division has been reignited by fears regarding the fragility of Northern Ireland's peace process (Hayes and McAlister, 2009a, 2009b). Low-level community violence and increased polarization in Northern Ireland have once more placed the spotlight on the separate school system. With calls for more integrated schools (Alliance Party, 2010), there are questions regarding the efficacy of community relations policy in education (Education and Training Inspectorate, 2009).

The Netherlands

The socio-historical context surrounding the issue of faith schools in the Netherlands shares three crucial features with that of the UK. First, both countries are essentially Protestant nations that discriminated against Catholics in the seventeenth and eighteenth centuries. Second, in the nineteenth century both countries lifted the restrictions on the Catholic faith and granted Catholics full citizenship, a series of events that in both countries became known as the Catholic Emancipation. Third, both countries acknowledge religious pluralism and share a tradition of state-supported faith schools (Walford, 2000). It is tempting to assign the two countries to the same group of liberal–pluralist countries on the basis of these similarities.

However, what makes the Netherlands quite different from the UK is the significant religious segregation that characterized Dutch society until well into the 1970s. This phenomenon, known as *Verzuiling* (pillerization), manifested itself not so much territorially as institutionally, with each religious and non-religious group (Catholics, the two main branches of Protestantism, liberals, and socialists) forming its own societies concerning almost every aspect of public life. Thus, from the end of the nineteenth century these groups began to establish their own schools, sport clubs, political parties, broadcasting corporations, and so on. This segmentation of society was greatly enhanced by the increasing political clout of the Catholics and the *Gereformeerden*, members of a strict branch of the Dutch Reformed Church, comparable to the Free Presbyterians (Lijphart, 1977). It was the alliance of these two groups that eventually managed to overcome liberal opposition to the idea of faith schools being financed with public means. The revised constitution of 1917 marked the end of a century-long *Schoolstrijd* (school battle) between these opposing sides. It sealed the victory of the confessional forces with the famous Article 23, which guaranteed full public recognition and financial support for the establishment and maintenance of privately governed denominational schools based on religious or ideological principles (Vermeulen, 2004). From this time, faith schools, such as Muslim institutions, and those based on certain pedagogical principles, for instance those of Montessori and Steiner, became fully state-funded, contrasting markedly with their equivalents in England, which were only partly state-funded (Francis and Lankshear, 2001).

Walford (2002) states that the reason for the establishment of new faith schools in the Netherlands is the disjuncture that many parents perceive between what they wish to teach their children in the home and the education provided by schools. Currently, there are 7,960 primary and secondary schools in the Netherlands, which include 2,408 public and 4,893 private schools (of these private schools 2,303 are Protestant, 2,322 are Catholic, and 741 are other private education institutions) (CBS, 2011).

France

The position of faith schools in France is related to its historical position vis-à-vis secularism in public institutions. In 1789, the events of the Revolution led to the Declaration of the Rights of Man and the Citizen, which weakened the power of the Catholic Church as much as other institutions of the *Ancien Régime* (*Declaration of the Rights of Man and Citizen*, 1789).

The church continued to play a key role in maintaining social stability and national loyalty in France during the nineteenth century. However, an increase in hostility between the church and state was brought to a head by legislation in 1905 (1905 Separation Act; see Gunn, 2004). The Separation Act signalled a change in direction and introduced a range of administrative and procedural measures that effectively entrenched church–state separation. The principle of secularism in education (Bloemberg and Nijhuis, 1993; Roelsma-Somer, 2008) was reaffirmed in the preamble to the 1946 French Constitution, later incorporated into the current 1958 Constitution:

> France shall be an indivisible, secular, democratic and social Republic. It shall guarantee equality before the law of all citizens without distinction according to origin, race or religion. It shall respect all beliefs.
>
> (French Constitution of 4 October 1958, Article 1).

In her discussion of faith schools in France, Deer (2005) states that religion, atheism, and agnosticism have played a central part in the political and intellectual shaping of the country. The educational reforms of the Third Republic at the end of the nineteenth century informed the basis of the definition of state schooling in constitutional terms and also inform today's debates about education in France. After the First World War, when the Republic became the established and accepted form of democratic government, 'the dichotomy between faith/private and secular/public schools became established not only as one aspect of the educational system but as one of its defining elements' (Deer, 2005: 180). See, for example, Ministère des Affaires Étrangères (2007), 'Secularism in France'.

Discussion of faith schools in France needs to be set within this historical context and the ongoing debate over the role of religion and the operation of secularism and secular institutions in public life. More recently, there has been controversy surrounding the wearing of the *hijab*, or head covering, by Muslim pupils (Parker-Jenkins, 2011). The *hijab* has become associated with social policies of integration and assimilation, despite the fact that many Muslim girls and women were born or have grown up in France.

The position taken by the French Government and public schools toward the wearing of the *hijab*, states Jones (2009a), is not simply a reflection of anti-Muslim sentiment nor even a recently devised attempt to target the Islamic headscarf. Rather, it represents a contemporary manifestation of a historical policy of secularism, the original purpose of which was to prevent religious and political ideologies and activities from influencing public school students and curricula. However, Muslims in France have argued that, despite expressions of secularism, the Catholic Church has been privileged over other faith groups and the pattern continues (Deer, 2005). In broader debates around dress and faith, Jones (2009a) notes that the 2004 legislation introduced in France – namely Article 1, Law No 2004-228, 15 March (Ministère des Affaires Étrangères, 2007) – effectively redefined secularism in a narrower sense, restricting and penalizing students' choices in relation to their clothing or manifestation of religious symbols, which potentially conflicts with the right to freedom of religious expression. In doing so, the law radically changed the previous legal regime, imposing an outright ban on the wearing of visible religious signs and eliminating the degree of judicial discretion and flexibility that administrative courts could exercise in assessing the circumstances of each case and reaching their decisions. As such, under the French law of 2004 (law 2004-228 of 15 March 2004) on secularism and conspicuous religious symbols in educational institutions:

> Muslim girls wearing the headscarf may be expelled from school whether or not they have engaged in political or proselytizing activities, disrupted teaching or disturbed public order.
>
> (Jones, 2009b: 16)

The original objective of the policy of *laïcité* (laicism) in France was to prevent (religious) indoctrination and promote religious equality. It could be said that this original objective has been forgotten, resulting in an excessively strict application of *laïcité* and, in a sense, a replacement of religious dogmatism with secular dogmatism.

Throughout this discussion we have noted the significance of personal and community identity based on religious education. Christian, Jewish, and Muslim schools have been established to ensure educational provision in conformity with parents' religious convictions, the ethos of the home, and the collective sense of identity. This need has become more apparent since the post-1960s period when immigration introduced large numbers of people contributing to a more culturally diverse society. It has been argued that France in particular has been struggling with this manifestation of religious belief in the face of what is viewed predominantly as a secular school system (Nielsen, 2004; Mookerjee, 2005; Hadden, 1989), and there has been a struggle to balance policies that protect secularism with those that protect religious identities. The 2004 law (Ministère des Affaires Étrangères, 2007) on secularism has changed the delicate judicial balance that French administrative courts, particularly the Conseil d'État, had worked to achieve throughout the 1990s. According to Jones (2009b), the law compromises rights that secularism and the Republic are supposed to uphold. This has significant implications for the doctrine of secularism in France and cultural and community values. As such, Jones maintains, the issue of banning the *hijab* can be judged negatively, as a suppression of the schoolgirl's right to manifest her religious beliefs by wearing the headscarf, or positively, as a protection of pluralism and secular cultural values. In France, these events constitute a modern-day challenge for secularism, signalling that there are important questions to be asked about the nature of contemporary secularism in society and the place of religion and schooling.

Summary

This chapter has provided a brief overview of the establishment of faith schools in England and Wales, Scotland, Northern Ireland, the Netherlands, and France. What these schools all share is a desire to perpetuate their respective religious/cultural identities through their organizational ethos, which in turn contributes to the raison d'être of their educational institutions. A number of themes have emerged including the allegation that faith-based education in a plural society allegedly leads to fragmentation, and Northern Ireland is cited as a key example. This is countered by supporters of religiously affiliated education who argue that faith schools are not antithetical to a harmonious social order; in some cases, they can promote social cohesion and help pupils perform well academically. This is what Putnam (2002) calls the process of bonding, which leads to bridging social capital with other organizations outside of one's own community. Lastly, the prevailing situation in France has traditionally been one of separation between church and state. Yet, the tradition of secularization in the public domain is being challenged by religious groups that wish to manifest their faith at school and beyond.

The theoretical background to faith schools and multiculturalism in the UK forms the basis of Chapter 2, where we discuss the complexities and tensions in responding to community needs and providing government policy based on national considerations.

Chapter 2
Faith schools and the wider community
Controversy and debate

In exploring how faith schools sustain group identity and maintain links with the wider community, we need to address the broader context of the ongoing debate on faith schools and their effects on community relations in general. The emergence of the UK community cohesion policy in the early 2000s placed this debate in the limelight, but the debate itself originates from the nineteenth century, when public education organized by the state started challenging the monopoly of the church. Delving into these wider debates, this chapter explores:

- empirical evidence of debates on faith schools;
- policy trends from the 1990s onwards and their consequences for the controversy surrounding faith schools;
- moves toward social integration and cohesion;
- and how our case study contributes to the discourse.

The debate on faith schools
The charges waged against faith schools in terms of their inability to promote social harmony are the same as the arguments that common school advocates use to further their cause. In brief, the latter hold that the common school, defined as a publicly-funded non-religious institution, promotes an overarching identity and a culture of learning by maintaining a neutral ideology and by enrolling children from a wide variety of social, ethnic, and religious backgrounds (Dewey, 1916; Feinberg, 1998; Pring, 2012). This 'ideological neutrality' is not understood as complete cultural relativism, but as a school ethos founded on several core values, including respect for diversity and equal treatment.

This diverse intake is further argued to foster more encompassing identities and an engagement with wider social issues, because the setting of the classroom is assumed to yield a harmony of aims, aspirations, and knowledge across social and ethnic groups. In short, having a multicultural classroom provides pupils with a greater ability to navigate different cultures and backgrounds. Ensuring that young people are constantly exposed to other beliefs, and exercising restraint in promoting a particular ideology, the common school creates the space for independent enquiry and allows pupils to arrive at a deeper understanding of the social world. Together, the qualities fostered by state-funded schools are seen as essential in underpinning the cohesion of liberal democratic societies.

It is on these points of socialization and student composition that the opponents of faith schools (for example Dawkins, 2001; Toynbee, 2001; British Humanist Association, 2002) base their arguments. Faith schools are accused of practising an all-encompassing (or 'thick') socialization, or – to use a stronger term – indoctrination, in that they ask students to accept certain religious beliefs as a totality of beliefs, values, and prescriptions, or more simply, as true and good (Halstead and McLaughlin, 2005). This allegedly can have the effect of numbing independent enquiry and promoting a narrow-minded outlook, which in turn could yield narrow sectarian identities and intolerant attitudes toward people of other persuasions (Vogt, 1997; Pring, 2005; Brighouse, 2006; see also the discussion in Haydon, 2009 and Everett, 2012). In short, because of the socialization they practise, faith schools are believed by some to promote a divided society composed of citizens with intolerant views toward other groups.

Faith schools are also thought by some to be divisive through their intake. The argument is that by their very nature they are serving particular groups of children, and even if they do not select on the basis of faith this will inevitably lead to segregation along religious and ethnic lines (Conway, 2009). In other words, opponents of faith schools believe that, by offering a 'restricted non-common educational environment … that is precisely intended for a particular group within society and not for society as a whole' (Halstead and MacLaughlin, 2005: 63), faith schools lead to 'educational apartheid' (Herbert 2001: 11). Indeed, it has been observed that Catholic, Jewish, and Muslim schools in Britain have a particularly homogeneous intake and have resisted plans by the British Government to reserve at least 25 per cent of places in state-maintained faith schools for children of all persuasions (Everett, 2012). In 2008, one particular Jewish school attracted considerable attention when it was taken to court by a parent claiming the school practiced racial discrimination in its admission policies (Hill, 2009) (we return to this Jewish Free School case later in the book).

Aligned with contact theory, there is a notion that isolation breeds prejudice (Allport, 1954; Pettigrew and Tropp, 2006); the opponents of faith schools argue that this segregation, in turn, fuels inter-group hostility and undermines a sense of commonality. Richard Dawkins (2001), for instance, contends that faith schools have played an important role in sustaining the sectarian divide in Northern Ireland. Similarly, a key report chaired by Ted Cantle (Independent Review Team, 2001; commonly known as the Cantle Report), while not referring explicitly to faith schools, sees the existence of separate institutions as supporting an environment where different ethnic and religious groups lead 'parallel lives', and argues that this is a key factor explaining the racial disturbances in the Northern English towns of Bradford, Burnley, and Oldham in the summer of 2001 (Independent Review Team, 2001: 9).

Conversely, advocates of faith schools have criticized the claim that these schools indoctrinate. McLaughlin (1996), for instance, has argued that many forms of religious education conform to the tenets of liberal democracy because they are based on religions characterized by 'openness with roots' (McLaughlin, 1996: 147). In his view this ensures that the schools serving these religions teach about 'the other', encourage dialogue, and thereby contribute to independent thinking and democratic citizenship.

At this point it is useful to introduce the typology of religious doctrine developed by Race and Hedges (2008). According to these authors, religions and branches within a certain religion can be distinguished by their understanding of salvation. Those entertaining an exclusivist conception of salvation believe that access to paradise is restricted to members of the faith. This conception is often associated with fundamentalist and intolerant sects. Respecting people of other faiths would, in this understanding of salvation, be unthinkable and immoral, as it would imply 'sentencing them to eternal damnation' (Everett, 2012: 46). Others have an inclusivist understanding of salvation, meaning that the best way to salvation is through the faith in question, but paths through other faiths are possible as well if these are part of God's plan. Finally, some faiths have a pluralist conception of salvation: one's own faith is only one among many equally legitimate trajectories to salvation.

McLaughlin's 'openness with roots' religions can be said to fall within these last two categories. They refer to religions welcoming members of other faiths and encouraging their members to open up to, and show a commitment to, wider society. According to Grace (2003: 152), the Catholic Church can be classified as inclusivist from the Vatican II reforms of the 1960s onwards, as these reforms have made the church 'more open to debate and dialogue and to relations with the wider society'. Hick (1995) agrees, and observes that the main Christian denominations in the UK today (the Church of England and the Catholic Church) can be considered inclusivist, serving the wider community and endorsing values compatible with liberal democracy. Indeed, a report commissioned by the Church of England observed that Anglican primary schools were doing as well as non-faith primary schools in reaching out to the wider community (Jesson, 2009). Using Ofsted data, it also found Anglican secondary schools to actually outperform non-faith secondary schools in countering discrimination and in promoting community cohesion and equal opportunities. However, some evangelical denominations, such as Pentecostalists and some branches of Islam 'are more likely to be found in the exclusivist category' (Everett, 2012: 46). This raises the question of whether faith schools serving these communities are capable of promoting independent enquiry, tolerant and inclusive attitudes, and engagement with the wider society.

The claim that faith schools, by definition, segregate has also been challenged. According to Bryk *et al.* (1993) it is precisely the social justice mission of Vatican II that motivates Catholic schools in America to serve the wider community in metropolitan areas and thus to open their doors to people of all kinds of persuasions and socio-economic backgrounds. Expanding on this, Grace (2003) concludes that contemporary Catholic schools in America stand out for their very diverse intake, socially, ethnically, and religiously. Similarly, in England, Anglican schools have traditionally served the wider community and are known for their very diverse make-up in large urban centres (Everett, 2012). Studies from the Netherlands also support the view that faith schools need not lead to educational apartheid. On the contrary, public secular schools are argued to be slightly more segregating as they mainly serve secular communities and are less appealing for ethnic minorities (Karsten, 1994; Dijkstra *et al.*, 2004). In the words of Dijkstra *et al.*:

> Still, many children of immigrant workers would prefer religious to public schools. This preference for religious schools is due in part to the greater openness of Catholic and Protestant schools to accommodating religious values, even those of religions other than their own, such as Islam.
>
> (Dijkstra *et al.*, 2004: 71–2)

In a further critique of anti-faith school rhetoric, Halstead and McLaughlin (2005) have questioned the assumed link between the promotion of a religious ethos in faith schools (that is, indoctrination) and intolerance. They argue that a sound moral basis may well have to be in place to support the ability to tolerate other religions:

> There is a sense, then, in which toleration presupposes being confident in one's own beliefs and values and having a clear self-identity. Perhaps this is just as important as actually being educated alongside children from different faiths and worldviews, and this is something that faith schools are well placed to provide.
>
> (Halstead and McLaughlin, 2005: 70)

They further argue that the cultural relativism fostered in (some) common schools leaves children feeling insecure and without a moral compass. By implication, such schools would not be in a good position to foster tolerant attitudes and behaviour. Akhtar (1993: 43) similarly argues that separate-faith schooling helps a minority experiencing a cultural threat to 'gain the confidence and security it needs in the early days of its establishment'. He postulates that this confidence, once attained, will eventually further the minority's integration into wider society.

It has also been noted that the proposed relation between segregation and prejudice – or, vice versa, the link between diversity and tolerance – is anything but a given. Kokkonen *et al.* (2010) and Janmaat (2012), for instance, have highlighted the limited value of contact theory in its classical form as proposed by Allport. Allport (1954) argued that intercultural contact can only be assumed to lead to more intercultural understanding and overarching identities if it occurs on the basis of equality, if it is frequent, lasting, and intensive, and if it involves common experiences and objectives and is closely monitored by a person in a position of authority. In diverse contexts where these conditions are not in place, cross-cultural interaction can actually yield opposite outcomes. Although the educational setting of the school meets many of these conditions, we cannot assume that culturally diverse schools will always generate higher levels of tolerance than ethnically homogeneous schools. Indeed, examining the civic values of young people in England, Janmaat (2012) and Keating and Benton (2013) did not find any positive link between classroom ethnic diversity and inclusive views on immigrants.

In addition to these theoretical critiques, a number of studies have also assessed more empirical critiques by exploring whether faith schools lead to greater prejudice and inter-group hostility. Research comparing mainstream Christian faith schools to non-faith schools in western societies generally has found either no difference or a difference in favour of the former. In the United States (US), Greeley (1998) found that Catholic youth attending Catholic schools were not only less prejudiced than public school students but they were also less prejudiced than Catholic youth in public schools. Another example concerns the research by Elchardus and Kavadias (2000) in Flanders (Belgium) among students enrolled in public and Catholic schools. Holding social background and achievement constant, as Greeley did, they found no difference between students in Catholic and public schools in their attitudes toward ethnocentrism and authoritarianism. In a sense these findings should not surprise us in view of the aforementioned evidence about the 'value-thin' socialization taking place in most Christian faith schools in western societies.

Interestingly, some research in non-western contexts also found that faith schools need not necessarily engage in the promotion of exclusionist and intolerant sectarian identities, as argued by the opponents of such schools. Exploring how schools engage with the issue of cross-sectarian social cohesion in Lebanon, Shuayb (2012) found that it was actually the non-faith public and private schools that shunned this issue and allowed no room for debate, primarily to maintain order and prevent conflict. In contrast, a number of private faith and secular schools addressed this issue comprehensively, as evidenced by their inclusive approach to student admissions and staff employment, extracurricular activities involving other faith groups, and democratic practices inside the school. She further found that students across the schools with these varying approaches to social cohesion did not differ in terms of their trust in people from other religions. The students in the schools with a more comprehensive approach to social cohesion expressed higher levels of trust in cross-sectarian secular parties and lower trust in sectarian parties (ibid.: 149).

Yet it would be premature to conclude that faith schools, whatever their type or location, are not divisive in any way. Very little is known, for instance, about minority faith schools, such as Jewish, Muslim, and Hindu schools. The little research available yields ambivalent findings. In comparing two Catholic, one Evangelical, one Muslim, and two non-faith schools in both the private and public sector in England, Everett (2012) found, on the one hand, no difference between levels of tolerance toward other religious and minority groups. On the other hand, she does note that in the Muslim school, students were considerably less accepting of members of their own faith violating religious prescriptions. This, she argues, may well have been the product of the 'value-thick' socialization practices in the school (involving restrictions on a critical examination of the Qu'ran), and of the perceived need to maintain intra-community cohesion in a wider secular society that views the Muslim community with suspicion. She emphasizes, however, that her findings concern a unique case and cannot be generalized to all Muslim schools in Britain.

This book builds on this research by exploring how a number of Jewish and Muslim faith schools are engaging with community cohesion. It will explore whether these schools have a segregating effect and will examine their school ethos and links with the wider community in order to determine the kind of socialization these schools are offering. The work is innovative in focusing not just on faith schools themselves, but also on the response of the wider community and the ways this response contributes to, or poses problems for, the maintenance of minority religious identity and for the interaction of the Jewish and Muslim faith schools with the outside world.

British trends from the 1990s: Whimsical government policy

What have been the policy trends of the last 15 years and how have these affected faith schools? What criticism have these policies evoked and how does our study address the shortcomings identified? These are the questions to be addressed in this section and throughout the book.

The expansion of maintained faith schools, in particular for minority faiths, was politically cemented by the formation of a new Labour government in May 1997. Up until 1997, all maintained faith schools were Christian or Jewish (*The Guardian*, 2001) but 17 years later there are also 11 Muslim, 4 Sikh, 1 Hindu, and 1 Greek Orthodox school (Inside Government, 2013a). Labour was keen to promote maintained faith schools, as they were believed to improve educational standards and formed a key element of the government's efforts to expand parental choice – a point we highlighted in the Introduction. They were also a symbol of the discourse on multiculturalism that prevailed in policy circles at the time. A key assumption of this discourse was that ethnic and religious minorities will only give their consent to the political institutions of the wider society on the basis of being appreciated and promoted by the state. The political integration of minority groups was thought to be achieved via a 'detour': they first need to be socialized in their own cultures before they can feel part of the receiving society (Berger *et al.*, 2004: 492).

In addition to raising educational standards, parental choice, and the recognition of minority faiths, the government was committed to combating exclusion, enhancing equal opportunities, and fostering the social and political participation of all groups in society. As a result, the Race Relations (Amendment) Act 2000 obligated schools to promote racial equality and eliminate unlawful racial discrimination from their own practice, and made citizenship education statutory in secondary schools. Citizenship education was expected to 'equip young people with the knowledge, skills and understanding to play an effective role ... in the life of their schools, neighbourhoods, communities and wider society as active and global citizens' (Education Act, 2002).

The post-9/11 era led the Labour government to rethink its policies on multiculturalism and integration. In brief, the change reflected a shifting emphasis away from the recognition and appreciation of diversity to the promotion of unity, shared values, and loyalty to British society, as captured in the new policy coined 'community cohesion' (McGhee, 2005; Flint, 2007). Cheong *et al.* (2005: 2) even labelled it as 'a return to assimilation'. The new policy was largely informed by two influential publications, commonly known as the Cantle and Ouseley reports, which asserted that racial segregation and the institutions maintaining it provide a fertile breeding ground for racial hostility, crime, and radicalization (Independent Review Team, 2001; Ouseley, 2001). Unintentionally, perhaps, these reports put the spotlight on minority faith schools, particularly those serving the Muslim communities, as possible nurseries of separatism, extremism, and fundamentalism. Indeed, in a controversial contribution, David Bell, the head of Ofsted, suggested that Muslim faith schools were taking insufficient action to socialize children in the norms and values of British society (Smithers, 2005). The new focus on community cohesion also reinvigorated the debate on faith schools more generally by giving a greater voice to the opponents of faith schools. Writers such as Alibhai-Brown (2000) and Young (2003) added to the misgivings by associating faith schools with a dysfunctional and diffusive multiculturalism erecting group boundaries and reifying minority cultures.

To clarify what the government meant by 'community cohesion' the Home Office defined it as:

> A shared sense of belonging based on common goals and core social values, respect for difference (ethnic, cultural and religious), and acceptance of the reciprocal rights and obligations of community members working together for the common good.
>
> (2001a: 18)

As we can see, this definition – alongside the emphasis on common values and an overarching identity – still includes the phrase 'respect for difference', which is reminiscent of multiculturalism. A notable omission from community cohesion policies is that they generally do not address deprivation, inequality, or exclusion. On receiving the Commission on Integration and Cohesion (COIC) report, which stated that 'integration

Faith schools and the wider community

and cohesion policies cannot be a substitute for national policies to reduce deprivation and provide people with more opportunities' (COIC, 2007: 21), the government modified the definition to incorporate these notions. Thus, in *Guidance on the Duty to Promote Community Cohesion*, the DCSF advised:

> By community cohesion, we mean working toward a society in which there is a **common vision** and **sense of belonging** by all communities; a society in which the diversity of people's backgrounds and circumstances is appreciated and valued; a society in which similar **life opportunities** are available to all; and a society in which strong and positive relationships exist and continue to be developed in the workplace, in schools and in the wider community.
>
> (DCSF, 2007a: 4; emphasis in original)

The Education and Inspections Act (2006) obliged all maintained schools to promote community cohesion from September 2007 onwards. Schools were free to fulfil this duty in ways they found most appropriate, and the aforementioned document offered various strategies and examples of good practice (DCSF, 2007a). From September 2008, Ofsted started to inspect schools using a given set of criteria to judge how well they performed this duty. We will discuss the concept of community cohesion further in Chapter 5 in order to advocate an alternative perspective: *community engagement*, which in our view represents a more bottom-up approach to documenting a school's interaction with the wider community.

Social integration and cohesion

The Conservative–Liberal-Democrat coalition government established in 2010 did not formally revoke the community cohesion policy, but its continued support for it can be said to be lukewarm at best. According to Rowe *et al.* (2011: 4), the government 'signalled its preference for achieving the integration of British ethnic minority communities through the Big Society narrative rather than that of community cohesion'. The Big Society initiative – which in the words of Prime Minister David Cameron involves 'taking power away from politicians and giving it to people' (Inside Government, 2013b) – captures notions of autonomy, strong civil society, providing for oneself, and *laissez-faire*. In contrast to the previous government, it assigns only a minimal role to the state in promoting integration and social cohesion. Hence, it comes as no surprise that the Secretary of State for Education, Michael Gove, expressed his intention to:

> ... sharply reduce the bureaucratic burden on schools, cutting away unnecessary duties, processes, guidance and requirements, so that schools are free to focus on doing what is right for the children and young people in their care.
>
> (DfE, 2010b: 9)

One of the victims of this drive to 'clean up bureaucratic excess' was community cohesion. As of 1 January 2012, Ofsted was no longer required to inspect schools on how well they performed this task (DfE, 2012a). Given this relaxation, schools could significantly be expected to take promoting community cohesion less seriously. However, what the new government crucially shared with the community cohesion agenda was a commitment to common values and 'Britishness', and a rejection of permissive multiculturalism. To underline its commitment to unity and security, it continued, for instance, the Prevent Strategy in a modified form (HM Government, 2011). This programme was set up by the previous Labour government to combat extremism and the radicalization of disadvantaged youth. It generated a widespread feeling in the Muslim community that they were identified as a 'suspect population' and could therefore be legitimately spied upon (O'Toole *et al.*, 2012; Lambert and Githens-Mazer, 2010).

Although this short review has shown how inconsistent government policy has been over the last 15 years or so, it has also identified one clear trend: the change from multiculturalism to the promotion of shared values and security as a means to enhance cohesion. It is precisely this shift, and the concurrent change from welcoming minority faith schools to viewing them with suspicion, that has attracted considerable criticism. Harrison (2004) and Flint (2007), for instance, warn that the emphasis on shared liberal values risks designating minority faith groups as the source of problems of cohesion and obscuring the role that power structures play in sustaining alienation and division. Burnett (2004) takes this critique to another level by arguing that the community cohesion policy represents a deliberate move by the government to criminalize ethnic minority youth and to maintain white privilege. He notes that the Cantle Report singularly focused on isolated communities as the cause for the outbreak of the violence in the summer of 2001, and consistently overlooked:

> the wealth of research documenting the discriminatory imposition of formal police powers upon certain Asian communities, the rising levels of unemployment and residential segregation within

certain Asian communities and the intrusion of an increasingly insistent far-Right ideology.

(Burnett, 2004: 10)

Burnett also accuses the Home Office policy makers of 'either ignoring or subverting [the] recommendations [of the Macpherson Report] on institutional racism' (ibid.: 10). In other words, the riots of 2001, in his view, were not caused by rising fundamentalism among minority faith groups but by a combination of the dominant group trying to maintain racial hegemony and the subordinate groups of colour no longer accepting being excluded and discriminated against. This notion of minority youth revolting against perceived injustice is echoed by Young (2003), who also claims that second generation immigrant youth, far from turning their backs on liberal values, have internalized western ideas of equal treatment and social justice. In his view, the dissatisfaction among this group and the outbreak of violence in 2001 has a lot to do with:

> the paradox that ... as the second generation become culturally closer to the 'host' and their economic and political aspirations concur with the wider society, at that point, they face both cultural exclusion because of racism and prejudice and become aware of the limits of their economic opportunities in the deprived areas in which they often live.
>
> (Young, 2003: 455).

Others would concur with the view that problems of community cohesion are driven by issues around social deprivation. A number of studies have found strong links between neighbourhood socio-economic status (SES) and key indicators of cohesion, such as interpersonal trust, civic participation, and attitudes toward out-groups. The lower the neighbourhood status, the more distrusting people are, the less they organize themselves, and the more hostile they are toward out-groups (Li *et al.*, 2005; Oliver and Mandelberg, 2000; Ross *et al.*, 2001, Letki, 2008; Laurence, 2011). Oliver and Mandelberg (2000: 576) explain this link by pointing out that low neighbourhood SES is invariably accompanied by 'petty crime, concentrated physical decay, and social disorder', and that this in turn leads people exposed to these circumstances to develop feelings of anxiety, powerlessness, alienation from neighbours, and suspicion toward outsiders. They further observe that economic hardship triggers inter-group competition over scarce resources, which only contributes to a hostile posture toward out-groups.

Letki's (2008) study is interesting, as it focused on England and Wales and used data from the Home Office *Citizenship Survey*, a nationally representative survey including data from over 15,000 individuals and 839 neighbourhoods. These data were collected between March and October 2001, which was precisely the time when the disturbances occurred in Bradford, Burnley, and Oldham. Letki also finds that when ethnic diversity and neighbourhood SES are put together in one explanatory model, only the latter shows a strong and significant link to various dimensions of social capital (neighbourhood attitudes, sociability, organizational involvement, and individual help). In other words, it is socio-economic deprivation that yields community breakdown, not diversity. In Letki's view, the reason diversity is often put forward as the culprit of social ills is that, in many cases, it coincides with deprivation. This coincidence and the way that the media report on social troubles lead people to 'racially code' offenders and welfare recipients, which 'results in the perception of diversity as undesirable' (ibid.: 121).

This concurrence of diversity and deprivation is precisely what characterized, and continues to mark, the environments where the disturbances erupted in July 2001. Oldham, Burnley, and Bradford stand out as working class areas with particularly high unemployment levels among the Pakistani and Bangladeshi communities (Bagguley and Hussain, 2008). Four of Oldham's wards are in the 100 most deprived out of a total of 8,400 wards in the UK as measured by the index of deprivation (Halsall, 2012: 82). The Cantle Report recognized this deprivation, noting the deep sense of disadvantage felt by some communities and the 'far from equal opportunities with respect to housing, employment and education' (Independent Review Team, 2001: 11). Yet it argued that the existing special arrangements and programmes aimed at tackling the needs of disadvantaged groups only reinforced a sense of grievance and thereby led to more division. It therefore called for a programme capable of 'busting myths', bringing people together, and fostering a greater sense of citizenship based on common values and principles (ibid.: 11–12).

Others, however, have suggested a more cynical reason for the eagerness among policy makers to embrace the recommendations of the Cantle Report, namely focusing on the self-organization of citizens and community cohesion as 'an attractive (and cheaper?) alternative for tackling social exclusion and regeneration [rather than costly social programmes]' (Forrest and Kearns, 2001: 139). This reason might apply all the more in the current age of austerity. Whatever the reason for the readiness of policy makers to heed Cantle's advice, the community cohesion policy, according to McGhee (2003), has marginalized earlier policy aimed at combating exclusion and deprivation, such as the aforementioned Race Relations Act.

In addition to scholars arguing that the real underlying cause of community breakdown is exclusion and deprivation, some question the assumption that having separate institutions for different minority faith groups contributes to division. Grace (2003) and Flint (2007) point out that a similar charge of divisiveness was waged against Roman Catholic schools in the US and Scotland in the early twentieth century, as we noted in Chapter 1. Regarding the latter, Flint quotes a committee of the Church of Scotland stating, in 1923, that these schools serving the poor Irish immigrant community would only divide Scotland racially, socially, and ecclesiastically. Yet this prediction has not materialized. From the moment Roman Catholic schools were integrated into the state sector in 1918, sectarian tensions have gradually diminished due to the success of these schools in eliminating the 'historical educational disadvantage suffered by Catholics of Irish descent in Scotland' and thus in reducing educational inequalities with the Protestant majority (ibid.: 261). Grace (2003) has noted that very similar reservations have been expressed against Catholic schools in the US historically. Yet, as noted before, Catholic schools in the US have actually been found to be conducive to supporting the common good, invalidating the criticism that they are divisive. These historical precedents suggest caution in accepting the dire consequences of minority faith schools as a given truth.

On the other hand, it would be premature to assume that the historical experience of Catholic schooling can be generalized to schools serving other religious minorities. We have already noted that reforms by Vatican II saw Roman Catholicism adopt a more inclusive understanding of salvation and consequently open up to wider society. If minority faiths have inflexible and exclusivist notions of salvation, to which they cling tenaciously, faith schools serving these communities may well be divisive. According to Hurst (2010), another reason that the historical trajectory of Catholic schooling may well be unique is that Catholicism is supported by a hierarchical structure of authority, which other religions and denominations, such as Islam and Evangelical churches, lack. It is this central authority that urged parents to enrol their children in maintained Catholic faith schools, 'ensuring a seamless continuity for parents between home, school and church' (ibid.: 96). In contrast, in the decentralized world of Islam there is no concerted effort to establish a network of maintained Muslim faith schools across the country. Rather, parents are able to send their children to the local *madrassah* (the mosque school) for religious socialization. The effort is on ensuring that the non-Muslim maintained schools to which Muslim parents send their children will take the religious sensitivities of these children into account.

Jewish and Muslim faith schools, as the focus of this book, share one crucial similarity with their Catholic predecessor: a sceptical if not sometimes outright hostile wider environment as discussed in Chapter 1. The aforementioned studies on Catholic schools have highlighted the resistance such schools had to cope with in Scotland and the US at the beginning of the twentieth century. Parker-Jenkins (2002) has noted the very same posture toward Muslim schools by showing the reluctance of the government, until the takeover by Labour in 1997, to grant Muslim schools a maintained status despite a considerable number of applications for such a status over a 15-year period. Yet the posture of the wider society toward the Muslim community is not manifested just at the policy level. It is also expressed in many social domains, including the media, local institutions, civic society, and life on the street. Following the attacks on the World Trade Centre on 9 September 2011 and the London Underground on 7 July 2005, this posture has clearly become more restrictive and reserved.

Our book assesses the stance of the wider environment in these domains and explores how Jewish and Muslim faith schools, in turn, respond to this posture. This is particularly important in view of the possibility, suggested by Everett (2012), that a hostile stance on the part of the wider environment, real or perceived, triggers a defensive reaction among minority groups, a reaction characterized by a strict maintenance of group cohesion and heavy policing of members internally. Choudhury *et al.* (2005) note the possibility that such hostility, in the form of Islamophobia, for instance, is even consciously constructed by the religious minority in order to perpetuate a siege mentality, cultivate a sense of victimhood, or quell legitimate criticism. A study of the response of Jewish and Muslim faith schools to (alleged) out-group hostility is all the more pertinent as, to our knowledge, none of the existing studies of Jewish and Muslim faith schools have addressed this issue head-on. Everett (2012) surmised that external hostility might account for the tight in-group bonding of the students in the Muslim school in her research (as expressed by their intolerance toward faith group members breaking the rules), but could not conclusively demonstrate this.

Conducting ethnographic fieldwork in an independent Muslim girls' school, Rizvi (2010) observed that the school consciously blended

Islamic education with the national curriculum and sought to emphasize similarities with the latter rather than differences. She also noted the many links the school maintained with the wider community through interfaith dialogues, visits to synagogues and churches, and community events such as campaigns and fund-raising events. The students attending the school were found to be of diverse national and social backgrounds. Most interestingly, they displayed a remarkable sense of agency as expressed in their active involvement in creating and recreating their 'British Muslim' identities, and in negotiating, choosing, or abandoning what they perceived as 'cultural' rather than 'religious' identities. These findings suggest that Muslim faith schools do not adopt a defensive inward-looking posture characterized by a strong disciplining of faith group members in response to a (perceived) hostile environment. In this light it is worth mentioning that the community of British Muslims can draw on some institutional support in its struggle against Islamophobia. The Islamic Human Rights Commission, for instance, has actively engaged with parents, community leaders, and schools to combat faith-based hostility. One of its strategies has been the provision of information packs with specimen letters challenging prejudice and verbal abuse (Choudhury et al., 2005). Yet, as Rizvi readily admitted, the school she researched may well not be representative of other independent Muslim schools. Further, it may be more difficult, even for researchers of Muslim backgrounds themselves, to gain access to schools that are more isolationist in their curriculum and school practices.

Neither historical nor contemporary research on faith schools serving minorities has found clear indications of such schools contributing to intergroup conflict. Nonetheless, we can conclude only tentatively that minority faith schools are not divisive, as there is so little research examining the interaction of such schools with the wider environment. Existing research has also, by and large, ignored the posture of wider society toward minority faith schools and the role this has played in heightening or diffusing tensions.

Summary

In this chapter we have explored the debates and controversies surrounding faith schools, and government policy aimed at developing a more integrated society. The abandoned policy of community cohesion has been reviewed together with the ill-explained replacement of the Big Society, which struggles to be understood or have visible impact. In the meantime, faith schools and others will continue to balance the need to adhere to their own priorities (in light of cultural and religious considerations) with reaching out to the wider community. In Chapters 3 and 4, we explore the significance of education from the perspectives of Jewish and Muslim faith schools, their own concept and development of 'community', and, drawing on our case study research, their strategies for reaching out and their experiences of hostility.

Chapter 3
Jewish concepts of community

> *Community values the 'we' as well as the I, it restores the dignity of agency and responsibility, and above all it tells us where to begin if we seek a better world.*
>
> (Sacks, 2000: 15)

Faith schools are part of the educational landscape in England and Wales, as elsewhere, reflecting an increasingly multi-cultural and multi-faith society. For the purpose of our discussion here we focus on two particular types of faith schools, based on Judaism and Islam, which have grown in number in the last 30 years and which are vulnerable to hostility from the wider community. Drawing on our case study of schools within these two traditions, we examine how faith schools situate themselves in contemporary society, maintain their religious-cultural heritage, and keep their communities safe.

In exploring these issues the chapter looks at:

- Jewish education in England;
- diversity within Jewish school communities;
- concepts of community within Judaism;
- the 2008 case study of faith schools;
- and experiences of anti-Semitism and issues of security.

Jewish faith-based education in England

The Jewish education system in the UK can be traced back to the mid-seventeenth century, as we noted earlier in Chapter 1, when day schools were established along with synagogues; in 1855, the first Jewish day school received state funding (Miller, 2007). Since then there has been an increase in the number of Jewish schools, particularly since the 1980s, in response to parental demand. Recent growth in Jewish school enrolment is part of a larger context of increased faith schooling provision in Britain (Valins *et al.*, 2001).

In terms of admissions to Jewish schools, policy has traditionally been based on the family's religious identity and affiliation to a synagogue. Recently, the UK Supreme Court reviewed this specific issue of admissions with reference to one of the oldest Jewish schools in England, the Jewish

Free School. The ruling over the Jewish Free School admissions policy (R on application of E v Governing Body of JFS and the Admissions Appeal Panel of JFS [2009] UKSC 15) changed the Jewish school landscape. Applicants for most mainstream Jewish schools now need to provide a Certificate of Religious Practice (CRP). This has had the effect of bringing many people back in contact with synagogues at a time when the growth of Jewish schools was sometimes blamed for their absence.

Dissatisfaction with the JFS ruling coincided with the emergence of a new grouping, the National Association of Jewish Orthodox Schools (NAJOS). Two organizations with similar purposes, the United Synagogue's Agency for Jewish Education and MST (a centre for training strictly orthodox teachers), both closed down. Similarly, Leo Baeck College's Centre for Jewish Education reduced its personnel and reviewed its involvement with schools. As a result, NAJOS has established itself as a voice for many schools in the strictly orthodox sector.

The government's introduction of a statutory duty to promote community cohesion for all state-funded schools (DCSF, 2007a) was greeted with ambivalence by some Jewish teachers. Some welcomed it as validating existing concerns and a stimulus to further activities, while others viewed the need to demonstrate the impact of their cohesion strategies as challenging. The JFS case rulings provided interesting new opportunities for schools and their local synagogues to work together. The CRP, devised at the recommendation of the Chief Rabbi, for example includes 'Gemilut Chasadim' – involvement with community activities – as one of the criteria for entry. A number of schools have developed very successful parent education programmes to help build bridges between classroom and home. This was an area that many members of the JLC's Schools Strategy Implementation Group felt should be expanded and supported further. They recognized that a Jewish school's remit goes far beyond teaching children during the school day (JLC, 2011).

Characteristics of Jewish schools

In terms of the characteristics of Jewish schools, these schools aim to inculcate Jewish values and traditions as interpreted by the local community as Judaism. Critical to this is the selection of a headteacher to provide appropriate leadership and to work in collaboration with the families to support the school. The headship of a Jewish school, as elsewhere, is part of a career development choice, but it carries with it support of the religious ethos. The changing nature of the role of headship has brought a change in outlook from both within and outside the school, and as in

Jewish concepts of community

other faith schools, such as those of a Christian tradition, headteachers in Jewish schools have to balance the academic aspects of education along with nurturing an appropriate ethos based on religious belief.

Similarly, the selection of a school curriculum is influenced by the nurturing of a Jewish ethos. The five recognized aims of Religious Education, required by state-funded schools (DfE, 2010a), are defined as understanding, values, community cohesion, world religions, and nurture, and schools respond to these aims in myriad ways. In faith schools there is often an emphasis on choice of clothing reflective of the school ethos – in other words, religion is expressed through clothing. Examples could include school uniforms carrying religious symbols or the *kippah* (head covering) in Jewish schools for boys and often skirts for girls. In some of the orthodox Jewish schools, separation of gender is integral to the school ethos, as is the practice in many Muslim schools, especially at secondary school level.

The community within both Judaism and Islam is built around specific texts. It is important to consider that sacred texts are to religious communities as 'research sources' are to secular environments. Within the Jewish faith, as in Islam, 'sources' are disembodied, atomistic, and the power derives from the content, whereas a 'text' is bound to a tradition and value is placed on who is speaking and in what context it is recognized. This notion is also related to community preservation, as a community is preserved by its texts, not subservient to its sources (Rapahal Zarum, personal communication, July 2012).

Involvement in both informal and formal Jewish education is detailed and nuanced (Graham *et al.*, 2014). In many Jewish communities, religious commitment is more important than intellectual content and rigour. Some argue that acculturation is more important than the knowledge itself, and skills are not just about training but self-actualization. Again, this resonates with other school communities based on a religious ethos.

Also relevant to this discussion is the controversy over what is being taught in Jewish and other faith schools and how this may contribute to indoctrination and extremism. Government school inspections have added to our understanding of faith schools and their level of moral as well as academic impact. A 2009 Ofsted study surveyed the spiritual, moral, social, and cultural development of pupils in 51 independent faith schools. While most schools were deemed 'fit for purpose', eight schools were found to be displaying teaching material biased toward one group. In a Jewish school, for example, a pupil's writing used strong language to describe events in the Middle East. Ofsted found that some of the *taqwa*-published material – that is, information from a Jewish publishing group – contained incorrect and biased information about other religions. Based on these findings, Ofsted recommended that the provision for citizenship be more clearly defined in legislation. As a result, a practitioner group was set up and non-statutory guidance on *Improving the Spiritual, Moral, Social and Cultural Development of Pupils* was produced (DfE, 2011). The issue of instilling appropriate moral and spiritual guidance concerns all faith schools and forms the basis of ongoing discussion and challenge. For Jewish schools, there is huge variance in how this is accomplished, due to the extent of differentiation within this group of schools.

Diversity within Jewish school communities

Diversity within Jewish school communities in the UK embraces a range of denominations, ethnicities, and cultures, for example institutions of orthodox, pluralist, and ethnic backgrounds, or Ashkenazi and Sephardi cultural heritage. Supplementary schools such as *yeshivas* and synagogue education, and affiliation to the Jewish Educational Trust or the National Jewish Agency, provide a different type of Jewish education.

Teachers act as role models, not just delivering information or pedagogical expertise. Various efforts in interfaith work often point to practices in education circles. Relevant literature on school improvement and teacher quality within Jewish schools points to a focus on teacher training and professional development in order to enhance teacher awareness of other faiths. New professional networks and development opportunities for teachers and school support staff have emerged through Partnerships for Jewish Schools (PaJeS), the Institute of Professional Development for Jewish Schools (IPDJS), and the Jewish Educators Network.

Parental choice of Jewish school is informed by parents' own Jewish background, and there is huge diversity within Jewish communities. In understanding Jewish differentiation, the role of the Board of Deputies is significant in categorizing Jewish denominations according to synagogues' affiliation (Graham and Vulkan, 2010). 'Strictly orthodox' as a classification includes synagogues within the Charedi Jewish community (ibid). Charedi Judaism is the most theologically conservative form of Judaism and is strictly adherent to *halacha* or Jewish law. *Halacha* guides every aspect of a Charedi lifestyle, from medical services to dress, educational systems to money, and family life to diet (Coffin and Bolozky, 2005; Lexilogos, 2014). Central orthodoxy is a 'modern and inclusive branch of Judaism, fully committed to the traditional practices of orthodoxy' (United Synagogue, n.d.). As a movement, it merges the observance of Jewish law and values with the secular, modern world – '*Torah im Derech Eretz*' ('Torah with the way of

Jewish concepts of community

the land'). Masorti Judaism as a whole is traditional, but ritual and practices differ from one community to another, particularly with regard to women's active participation in services (Masorti Judaism, 2013). It also validates a multifaceted approach to Jewish life, and aims to encourage enquiry and debate. *Gemilut hesed* (kindness) and *tzedakah* (charity) are key values of the Masorti movement. Beyond these Jewish denominations is Reform Judaism, an evolving faith that conserves Jewish tradition while keeping an open, positive attitude to new insights and changing circumstances (Reform Judaism, 2013). Ritually, Reform Judaism is egalitarian; men and women can sit together in the synagogue and women are included in a *minyan* (a gathering for religious obligations or rituals such as a prayer service). Modern ethics and values play a crucial role in Reform Judaism, especially democracy, human rights, and social liberalism.

Liberal Judaism was founded in the UK in the early part of the twentieth century and is the sister movement of Reform Judaism in North America. It is a distinctly progressive movement that 'affirms the dynamic, developing character of our Jewish religious tradition' (Liberal Judaism, 2012). It is a fully egalitarian movement that stresses the inclusion and involvement of men and women in all aspects of Jewish life and ritual. Liberal Judaism places a strong emphasis on ethical conduct and sees *tikkun olam* (repairing the world) as a fundamental mission for all Liberal Jews. It primarily uses English in its services and uses organ music to create a more inclusive form of worship (Liberal Judaism, 2012). Finally, Sephardi Jews are descended from Jews who lived in the Iberian Peninsula and still follow the customs and traditions of the region (Spanish and Portuguese Jews' Congregation, 2013). As a result, Sephardi Judaism is a distinct cultural tradition rather than a separate denomination. As we indicated in Chapter 1, regardless of nomenclature, accountability is required, and this takes place through an internal inspection called the Pikuach framework, which mirrors Ofsted and monitors and evaluates Jewish schools.

Having identified the major Jewish denominations it is important to note that within the umbrella term 'Jewish schools', these differences are reflected in their recruitment of pupils. Jewish schools in the UK tend to differentiate themselves through nomenclature, such as Masorti, reform, liberal, progressive, pluralist, ultra orthodox, or Zionist, depending on the communities' interpretation of Jewish identity. (We selected schools for our case study within this categorization, as explained later in this chapter.) Both primary and secondary numbers of Jewish schools have risen significantly over the past three years. The estimated number of Jewish schools in the UK as of 2013 (DfE, n.d.) is demonstrated in Table 1.

Table 1: Maintained and independent faith schools by religious character (as of May 2013)

	Jewish Schools		Muslim Schools	
	Primary	Secondary	Primary	Secondary
Voluntary Aided	27	6	6	5
Academy Converters	3	4		1
Free Schools	3		1	2
Free Schools (Proposed)	2	1		
Non-Maintained	1	1		
Total Maintained	47		15	
Independent	49		139	
Total Number of Schools	**96**		**164**	

Source: AMS UK (2014); DfE (n.d.); Find a Jewish School (n.d.); Scott and McNeish (2012)

Jewish concepts of community

The evolution of communities, whether supported by the state or not, is relevant to our understanding of how school communities outline the boundaries of inclusion and exclusion. This also involves how teachers understand the term 'community' within a school. Within Judaism, there are a number of different words for the concept of 'community', each with a slightly nuanced meaning. Some key terms that help to outline this concept from a Jewish perspective include *kehilla* and *eruv*. The term *kehilla* refers to an organization of a Jewish population for communal and charitable purposes. Further, geographical space is an important element within Jewish concepts of community. An *eruv* is an urban area enclosed by a wire boundary that symbolically extends the private domain of Jewish households into public areas, permitting activities within it that are normally forbidden in public on the Sabbath. A certain distance from the synagogue is delineated by a physical boundary, rope, or string to help to define a boundary around a community.

Reaching in, or building a 'cohesive' community where learning is paramount to driving successful students, is strengthened by ethos, heritage, and knowledge, and this is part of the nurturing community. From a Jewish perspective, Sacks maintains:

Community values the 'we' as well as the 'I', it restores the dignity of agency and responsibility, and above all it tells us where to begin if we seek a better world. For some time I have felt the ever urgent need for a national conversation to seek a more effective interaction between our schools and families, governments and local communities – between our institutions and our local sources of moral energy.

(2000: 15)

Efforts to retain and enrich religious–cultural identity within Jewish school communities happen in a number of ways, such as inviting parents to be partners, shared decision-making, outreach work, and linked activities. The internal efforts to create a cohesive community are met with a vision and rules around how to engage outside of these school communities. Teachers have greeted the government's introduction of a statutory duty to promote community cohesion with ambivalence; the Jewish community answers to the definitions and interpretations around 'community' through the positioning statement *Jewish Schools and Cohesion* (JLC, 2008: 55). Despite this we identified examples of reaching out to other communities, both religious and non-religious, which we discuss in Chapter 5.

This religious concept of a *kehilla*-centered approach to school is seen as a reciprocal interaction between the individual and the people and settings in which an individual finds him or herself within the course of daily activity. These developmental contexts are defined both on a micro level – people with whom and settings within which the individual interacts directly (such as a teacher in a classroom) – and more broadly, as systems that include the individual but with which he or she has no direct contact (such as the school governing board, parents of school friends, and so on).

Families and communities are not institutions but schools are, and they therefore have certain challenges when attempting to build an environment where learning flourishes. The literature demonstrates that building social capital supports learning (Coleman, 1994; Pugh and Telhaj, 2007). School-based strategies to secure engagement in learning are one aspect that supports building social capital *within* a school. The school community 'reaches in' and engages with parents. Schools may also 'reach out', for example organizing regular visits for people from outside the school to support and showcase it. The dominant models of education in the UK focus on relationships (Desforges, 2003) in which students learn, and Jewish schools are strongly built on similar notions of relationship.

We illustrate examples of 'reaching out' of the Jewish school community in the next section. An overview of our case study (Parker-Jenkins, 2008) was presented in the introductory chapter. Of the nine schools involved, four were based on Judaism. They constituted two modern orthodox Jewish schools, one at primary level, which was state-funded with VA status, and another at secondary level operating as an independent school. The remaining two were pluralist Jewish primary schools, and all were based in London and the Home Counties, reflecting the settlement patterns of Jewish communities. Over fifty stakeholders were involved, including pupil focus groups, parents, teachers, rabbis, and community representatives.

We found from our case study research (Parker-Jenkins, 2008; Parker-Jenkins and Glenn, 2011) that these communities were, alongside Muslim school communities, vulnerable to experiences of hostility from the wider community, and therefore making visits outside the school, or bringing people in, was arranged on the basis of appropriate security. For example, in all of the Jewish schools in our case study, security personnel were present, paid for by parents to ensure the community was safe; this is not the normal practice in the majority of community schools. We now highlight some of the perspectives obtained based on the key issues of hostility, anti-Semitism, and issues of security. For the purpose of discussion here we draw on evidence from our case study of hostility and anti-Semitism pertaining to Jewish schools, and follow this up in the next chapter with discussion and evidence of Islamophobia.

Experience of anti-Semitism and issues of security

Our case study found evidence of hostility toward students and a lack of acceptance among the wider community. Significantly, we found that hostility from the wider community was experienced more by children, rather than adults, who frequently dismissed or underplayed the issue. We explored these findings further and noted how the community adopted self-segregation approaches and heightened security arrangements as protection from external hostility.

Probing this point further, adults in the study would list incidents of hostility, such as verbal abuse outside school. Similarly, male pupils reported hiding the name of their school on their blazer when on public transport because they were afraid of bullying, and said they had received derogatory comments about their male circumcision. In this instance, we are not talking about simple bullying: anti-Semitism and racism is different from common forms of bullying between children. There is a fine line here, but bullying

Jewish concepts of community

with reference to circumcision is a specific attack on a person's Jewishness, distinct from other types of bullying (European Monitoring Centre on Racism and Xenophobia, 2009). One headteacher from a pluralist Jewish primary school was convinced of overt prejudice, saying, 'There is lots of evidence of anti-Semitism in the wider society'.

Leading scholars, noting the complexity of the area, define anti-Semitism as follows: 'a certain perception of Jews, which may be expressed as hatred toward Jews' (European Monitoring Centre on Racism and Xenophobia, 2009: 1). Julius (2010), a forthright expert on English anti-Semitism, argues that contemporary anti-Semitism has shifted the focus of attack on Jews. Since the late 1960s, he argues, a new type of anti-Semitism has emerged which conflates anti-Semitism with anti-Zionism and treats the State of Israel as an illegal Jewish enterprise. Many authors highlight the blurred boundary between political and religious discrimination. This was reflected in our case study in terms of school security:

> There is that other layer, that we are a Jewish school, and it is about doing it in a way which says we want school to be safe, we want the children to be safe but we are not scare-mongering. We do have a security officer and we take it very seriously.
>
> (Headteacher, modern orthodox Jewish school)

A parent–governor noted on this issue:

> When it was set up as a Jewish school we were told we had to have security. Originally it was going to be done by parents but that was never going to happen. In the end it was suggested that the parents put in extra money in their voluntary contribution so that we have a paid, hired security guard.
>
> (Parent-governor, pluralist Jewish primary school)

Asked whether this was as a result of any particular incident she said: 'No, because it a Jewish school and that is what Jewish schools do.'

Children were being targeted in a way that again appeared to be more than bullying between children, as we noted earlier in the chapter, and they may be affected by xenophobia, anti-Semitism, and racism. Importantly, it may not always be clear to the adult world what is going on. Instead it may be something that is just between children, sparked off by their school uniforms, or an incident on the way to school. If children are being targeted in this specific way, we need to consider how it may be repeated in other ways, and how improving the context of learning in all schools might be

57

addressed. One headteacher of a Jewish school provided an explanation about the situation with reference to the wider community:

> This was a huge council estate which was built after the war, and they had to house a lot of people, so they built a lot of new towns ... it was filled with white working class people. Very National Front, very racist ...What we have got [here is] two communities living intermingled with each other that are very different. The way the Jews have dealt with it is by not mixing with their neighbours, so they don't send their children to the local school round the corner. Two Jewish schools have opened in the area, and the Jewish don't mix with their neighbours.
> (Headteacher, VA modern orthodox Jewish primary school)

This issue of 'self-segregation' (Denham, 2001) was pursued further:

> What I am saying is that we work very hard to have our children mix with their neighbours, but our parents have chosen very strongly not to have their children educated with them, so they choose this school, partly because of the Jewish vision, but the main reason the parents choose this school is because we have nice children here, they mix with other Jewish children.
> (ibid.)

When clarifying whether this is a form of self-exclusion, the headteacher of a pluralist Jewish school replied 'absolutely'.

The notion of 'community' plays a part in how school communities respond to this concern. The framework for how schools can incorporate activities promoting community cohesion into their curriculum incorporates the view that twenty-first-century skills define the future success of students. Cohesion within a faith is an important factor expressed in bridging and bonding activities within schools (West-Burnham, *et al.*, 2007). As a headteacher of a modern orthodox school explained:

> We are very conscious of thinking of the wider community on three levels: (i) the Jewish wider community ... that includes Orthodox, Ultra Orthodox, Non-observant, Progressive, Liberal; (ii) a wider community, other faiths, and then (iii) a wider general community – English society in its multicultural mixed-up self.
> (Headteacher, modern orthodox Jewish school)

Anti-Semitism and Islamophobia are different manifestations of racism and can be viewed as a hostility toward strangers that includes discrimination on the basis of religion, race, and ethnicity (Weller, 2011). They are both contemporary racisms, mutations of changing historical circumstances and the deep-seated psychological fear of difference (Werbner, 2012). Hostility is a real challenge to engagement and broader social cohesion. From our case study we found that children are more vulnerable than adults to incidents of Islamophobia and anti-Semitism, yet little research or evidence uncovers this; incidents go unreported or stay between children and parents. This has implications for the way cohesion is to be understood and practiced in school communities.

The experiences of Jewish school communities and the challenges they face undermine or threaten efforts at greater community cohesion and engagement. Jewish school communities seek to maintain internal community coherence and protect against threats of identity erosion and other forms of hostility and xenophobia. Our case study of schools found that a number of key overlapping issues emerged which were layered and complex, related to the experience of hostility and the challenges of keeping themselves safe from the wider community. Security for Jewish schools in the UK is taken very seriously, guided by an organization called the Community Security Trust (CST, 2012), which respondents frequently cited (Parker-Jenkins, 2008).

We noted that before gaining access to the school we had to pass through a number of security measures, including a security officer and three doors, similar to arrangements we found in Muslim schools. When asked whether the level of security in the school was about anti-Semitism specifically, the headteacher of one pluralist Jewish primary school suggested they were prepared for hostility from any quarter and not just outside of their own group. The CST (2013), which informs their security arrangements, is an organization that specifically monitors and advises on anti-Semitism in broader society. We asked if this arrangement was a demand or an expectation of parents.

> No, it is not that, you would find that in any Jewish school. Basically there is the CST ... and they are the central organization for security in the UK and one of their people who works for them is responsible for all the Jewish schools, so we take advice and guidance from him as to how secure we should be.
> (Headteacher, pluralist Jewish primary school)

When asked whether the level of security in the school was about anti-Semitism specifically, she continued:

> It is, but it is more so. If you went to the school next door you have to press the buzzer and say who you are. You wouldn't be faced with CCTV cameras. This is what we have been advised to do ... I would go as far to say all Jewish schools in this country have CCTV cameras, they may not be quite as sophisticated as what we have got but ... I think that there is a double message; we want the children to be safe regardless of it being a Jewish school and having people at the gate. I mean I get e-mails possibly 2 or 3 a month saying just beware that a child was approached or this person has come in to a school, this is from the authority not from CST, so we have to be vigilant all of the time.
>
> (ibid.)

For some of the children, travelling by themselves outside of this 'social community', there were negative experiences. Some teachers challenged whether these hostile incidents were in fact based on anti-Semitism/Islamophobia or simply constituted 'normal' behaviour among school children. Similarly, there was a difference in opinion as to what constituted hostility or a security issue. For example, adults in the study would point to security as far as the safety of the school building was concerned, or people entering the property without security clearance, but not with regard to the issue of verbal bullying or what might take place externally. Yet, children reported having to deal with verbal abuse outside their school and when they travelled on public transport. For example, one Jewish teacher argued:

> I'm not surprised in the slightest that it does happen, but at the same time I wonder what these Jewish children on the buses are doing to wind other children up? I am Jewish and I'm all for Jewish people but at the same time they can't be just sitting there quietly. I don't believe they are. Confident Jewish kids think they are it. I am sure they do wind people up ... Are they, Jewish kids, sitting on the bus saying 'you f'ing Christians'?
>
> (Teacher, pluralist Jewish primary school)

This view that bullying is standard behaviour may underplay the xenophobia experienced by children. From a Jewish perspective, a teacher in a Jewish VA modern orthodox primary school said that pupils might raise questions in school, 'sometimes to do with Israel or the problems in the Middle East'. Probing as to whether anything had happened in their school community that was deliberately anti-Semitic in nature, she added:

> You get the occasional comment made in the street perhaps; someone may say 'Dirty Jews' or 'Yid Lid'. We report everything; we have to report every racist incident. Likewise we also take [into account] any racist comments within the school. Since I have been here there have only been two racist incidents with the children.
>
> (ibid.)

Asked whether this school was different and whether other schools were affected, the interviewee responded:

> I think it's a lot more when they get to secondary school, when they are travelling to and from school on their own, when they are at the shopping mall on their own, here they go everywhere with their parents, or they go to play football that's supervised.
>
> (ibid.)

This was validated by children in the focus groups who experienced hostility outside of school once no longer in adult company, and when at secondary school. One female Jewish teacher said:

> Anti-Semitism, we don't actually discuss it as such, we learn about the Holocaust, we are going to do a big project on it. We have Holocaust Memorial Day that's a national thing. … I don't think many of the children come across anti-Semitism on their day-to-day lives. If it exists it is very subtle, too subtle for them to pick up on.
>
> (Teacher, modern orthodox primary school)

However, she added:

> It's being proactive rather than reactive, and I think that is what is important about security. You can't wait until something happens before you do something … it is not a culture of fear, it is just a recognized culture within Jewish schools all over.
>
> (ibid.)

This contrasts with the experience of children in the same school who felt secure inside their school communities but vulnerable beyond the school gates. For example, one pupil in a focus group told us of an incident that had happened to a family when they were home, and their house was attacked by individuals they took to be non-Jews in a 'very, very Jewish area'. Similarly, the children reported their vulnerability when outside of school and travelling on buses. They revealed they were afraid to show the name of their school or let the school colours indicate which school they attended. A female teacher confirmed this sense of fear with reference to her own generation:

> I have friends that went to big Jewish schools, but they all travelled down together, they were in a big group. They were probably a bit intimidating themselves. I think from a Christian or Jewish school, [I] don't think it makes a difference.
>
> (Teacher, pluralist Jewish primary school)

Pursuing this question of whether such incidents happen in all schools, she responded:

> I think these things go on ... if it wasn't a Jewish school and it was a school for something else, they will find a reason, and other people will find a reason to fight their school.
>
> (ibid.)

The idea of tension between schools being quite normal was discussed with other community members, and the view was raised that the bullying that children reported may not necessarily be interpreted as anti-Semitic but just 'standard stuff' going on between kids. One primary school headteacher commented: 'I don't think that the kids really understand it, they don't understand what anti-Semitism is at that age'. When we shared with her the fact that some children told of being called 'you f'ing Jew', she said 'yes, that is anti-Semitic'. Other comments these children received included 'you have a circumcised penis' which again suggests it was deliberately anti-Semitic. Where do you draw the line between 'normal' and racist bullying that happens between children? She stated:

> Are they using the fact that they are Jewish as a weak spot ... finding their weak spot? But what are the Jewish kids doing back, what are their weak spots? ... I'm just playing devil's advocate ... I remember what some of the Jewish friends used to be like on the bus and some of the things that I heard, and the language I heard.
>
> (Headteacher, pluralist Jewish primary school)

This attitude suggests that previous generations have received similar verbal abuse. Interestingly, this teacher said, 'I haven't felt any anti-Semitism ... I leave here at 3 o'clock, so don't really come across it'. The fact that she left in a car was a factor in her perception, and a distinguishing feature we found between adults and older children who travelled to and from school by public transport and journeyed into the external environment by themselves. For example, one parent reflected:

> As far as my son is concerned, yes he does come home occasionally, not from school but from other activities, and he does mention the fact that he has been picked upon because he is Jewish. They ask him 'are you Jewish?' and he says yes and then they start to make comments about it. I did grow up in this country and I suffered it as well.
>
> (Parent, pluralist Jewish primary school)

Incidents of anti-Semitism in the UK are catalogued by the CST, and some are also cited by the Equality and Human Rights Commission (2011). While the number of anti-Semitic incidents has fluctuated since 2000 (peaking in 2009), the general trend has been upwards, and the 2010 figure was the second highest recorded since 1984 (CST, 2010: 10). The Equality and Human Rights Commission (Weller, 2011) highlights the persistence and dangers of anti-Semitism and outlines the complexity of these trends. Similarly, the Runnymede Commission report, *A Very Light Sleeper*, examined the incidences of anti-Semitism in the 1990s. Approaches to the relationships between anti-Semitism, anti-Judaism, and more general understandings of discrimination on the grounds of ethnicity and/or of religion have been complex and sometimes contested. Our case study found evidence to substantiate this report in the form of verbal attacks and the experience of hostility from the outside community, particularly among children.

Summary

This chapter has drawn on research from our case study examining the provision of education based on Jewish principles and highlights Jewish concepts of community. Differentiation within Jewish communities was explored together with the nature of Jewish schools. Issues of hostility and security were also examined. The schools in this study were operating on a number of levels: religiously, culturally, and academically in response to parental choice and expectations. Differences existed between primary and secondary schools in that as soon as children were able to travel by themselves to school they were more vulnerable to hostility from others in the form of bullying and anti-Semitic verbal assaults. The school stakeholders themselves questioned whether incidents of hostility constituted anti-Semitism, but nevertheless ensured they had security in place. They were cautious about the potential for hostility from the external community, and were made aware of security concerns through the existence of financial support for employing security personnel and measures at a level not normally used by other schools in the country. How some Muslim schools provide education and respond to concepts of community is explored in the next chapter.

Chapter 4
Muslim schools and concepts of community

O my Lord increase me in knowledge.

(*Al-Quran*, 20: 114)

There is great diversity within Muslim communities globally with regard to traditions, denominations, and cultural backgrounds. This diversity is reflected in the provision of what is considered an appropriate Islamic education. The different models and methods employed in Muslim schools in England point to attempts to develop an Islamic ethos and raise academic standards. At a broader level, Muslim schools nurture a sense of 'community' and choose the extent to which they link with the wider community. This chapter explores these issues with reference to:

- Muslim education in England;
- diversity within Muslim schools;
- concepts of community within Islam;
- and experiences of Islamophobia and security.

Muslim Education in England

Faith schools based on an Islamic ethos in England are identified under the collective term 'Muslim school', although there is huge differentiation within them based on sectarian and cultural factors (Halstead, 2007; Parker-Jenkins *et al.*, 2005; Parker-Jenkins, 2008). Elsewhere they are known as 'Islamic schools', as in the case of the Netherlands (Walford, 2001). Muslim schools are aligned with various *maslaks* (denominations), for example Deobandi and Barelvi (Lewis, 1994), and include Shia schools. *Darul Uloom* Muslim schools, for example, provide education with a particular emphasis on educating imams and religious leaders for the future.

We noted this diversity in Chapter 1, as well as the fact that faith schools established on Islamic principles have existed in England since the immigration of the 1960s and the increased dissatisfaction with community school provision (Hewer, 2001; Parker-Jenkins, 1995, 2002; Parker-Jenkins *et al.*, 2007). The needs of Muslim students in general include proximity to family, access to religious instruction, education in a safe environment that will lead to high academic attainment, and resources adapted to a Muslim ethos and in keeping with parental expectations.

Muslim leadership, as defined by the literature, refers to both religious leaders and school leaders or educationalists. The term 'Muslim faith leaders' is a broader term than 'imams'. The term 'imam' refers to a leader of a Muslim community, commonly used in the British context in connection with mosque imams who lead prayers, teach children reading the Arabic *Quran*, and lead religious rituals, for example marriages, funerals, and births. Further:

> The term 'imam' has different meanings and implications in Shia and Sunni Islam, and in Sunni Islam most Muslim faith leaders known as imams are based full-time or part-time at a mosque.
> (Communities and Local Government, 2010: 10)

Faith leadership is assumed not only in mosques but also in educational institutions, universities, conferences, and youth settings. Within Muslim communities, leadership is also exercised by teachers, youth workers, and spiritual and community leaders, including women members. To focus only on imams omits the significant leadership roles exercised by many others. As such, 'the term *Muslim faith leaders* is substantially more inclusive' (ibid.).

At present, the religious education provided in the majority of Muslim institutions for the 11– 19 age range is not accredited outside Muslim communities (AMS UK, n.d.). Some of the strongest evidence pointing to successful schooling is the quality of teaching and quality of leadership, and the positioning of some Muslim schools in national league tables. Indeed, pressure to provide government funding for Muslim schools in 1998, in keeping with other faith schools in the country, was due to the demonstrated academic success of these institutions (Parker-Jenkins, 2002). The development of teaching and leadership standards has shown a strong commitment to wider conversation and debates around National Standards, in faith-based schooling particularly. Eleven Muslim schools in England have been brought into the mainstream education system with government funding under the VA category, and the majority operate as independent institutions (Gov.uk, 2014). Funding for training and professional development of school leaders in England is evolving in terms of accreditation and recognition. Accreditation for teachers from faith backgrounds is on the increase. There are also *madrassah* schools providing supplementary Islamic education, normally outside of the school day, and which we discuss later in the chapter. While Muslim schools are now an established part of the educational landscape in England, there are practices

Muslim schools and concepts of community

that strengthen internal Muslim community life and efforts to reach out beyond Muslim communities:

> The sense of community in Islam extends from the local level of the family to the worldwide community of believers (umma). What binds the community together is the equality of all believers in the eyes of the divine law (sharf'a) ... In Islam, social existence has exactly the same goal as individual existence: the realization on earth of divinely ordained moral imperatives. Indeed, the spiritual growth of the individual (taqwa) can take place only within the shari'a.
>
> (Halstead, 2004: 523)

The constructed and contested nature of Muslim identity and religious activity is linked to how we understand the forming of relationships and views toward social capital. The ways in which individuals relate to tradition and community also have an influence on the concept of identity and citizenship (Halstead, 2009), as well as on their sense of belonging within a UK context (Modood, 2010; Seddon and Ahmad, 2012). This relates to how adherence to Islam influences the lived experience (Knott and McLoughlin, 2010). Muslim schools adapt and develop curricula to provide for their perceptions of identity, with religious events during school time such as 'Friday prayers', and an emphasis on Islamic principles that affect everyday life. The Muslim schools in our case study (Parker-Jenkins, 2008) were adapting the National Curriculum to reflect the school ethos or engagement in curriculum development. For example, the National Curriculum in English was followed, but their choice of literary texts was on the basis of Islamic sensibilities. Similarly, the selection of books in the library and access to Internet sites were also governed by Islamic considerations. There was also reference made by practitioners in some of the Muslim schools in our case study, who were affiliated with AMS UK, to the use of curriculum developed by similar institutions, such as those in South Africa, via transnational networks (AMS UK, n.d.; Muslim Directory, n.d.). As well as developing a knowledge base within each school, there were also a variety of ways in which the nurturing of relationships was taking place both within and beyond the school. The emphasis on 'bonding social capital' (Coleman, 1994; Pugh and Telhaj, 2007) assists in promoting shared values within the school community and a cooperative practice between the school and the home, which is perceived as lacking in non-faith-based schools. The development of social capital is a reoccurring theme in the literature on the establishment of Muslim schools in the UK and elsewhere, where there is compatibility in values and expectations (Hewer, 2001; Nielsen, 2004; Parker-Jenkins *et al.*, 2005).

Discussion of Muslim schools in England and elsewhere invariably includes mention of gender and particularly dress and behaviour expectations for women and young girls. The requirement for females, commonly over the age of 11, to wear a *hijab* or head covering has a religious connection:

> The Muslim woman is required to conceal her attraction from men by a strictly modest, straight forward type of attire ... outside her homeland at any time that she is in the presence of non-mahrem non-relatives ... she is required to wear a covering-type of dress which will make it clear to anyone who sees her that she is a chaste, modest and pure woman.
>
> (Haneef, 1979: 156)

A Muslim woman's *mahrams* form the group of relations who are, for example, allowed to act as escorts when she travels and when she will be particularly exhibiting modesty in dress (Abdul-Rahman, 2007).

Importantly, there is no consensus among Muslim communities about the requirement for Muslim women and young girls to cover themselves, nor about whether it is a religious or cultural/social class requirement, and this remains a contested area (Werbner, 2001). However, Muslim schools in England tend to have the *hijab* as part of their dress code (Parker-Jenkins, 1995, 2011), and within the Muslim schools in our case study (Parker-Jenkins, 2008; Parker-Jenkins and Glenn, 2011), all of the female students were expected to abide by this requirement, including the female teachers of Muslim background. The manifestation of religious identity in the form of increased wearing of the *hijab* can be understood in the context of public forms of identity as well as being a public statement of minority resistance to the dominant culture (Halstead, 2007; Shah, 2012). The wearing of the *hijab* features as a recurring and contested aspect of debates on multiculturalism in the UK and elsewhere, where it reflects institutional regulations governing dress code, as revealed in our research, or an expression of identity among Muslim women and their communities.

In our case study (Parker-Jenkins, 2008; Parker-Jenkins and Glenn, 2011), the *hijab* was often cited by Muslim girls as being the focus of attention and attracting negative comments from the wider community. As Finney and Simpson observe:

> The point here is not that there is debate about diverse practices but that minorities, and particularly Muslims, are singled out

as having behaviours potentially undesirable for British society, and that the responsibility for ensuring they "fit in" lies with the minorities themselves.

(2009: 95)

The controversy is not restricted to the UK. In broader debates around dress and faith in France, Jones (2009a) notes that legislation enacted in 2004 effectively redefined secularism in a narrower sense, as we noted in Chapter 1. Jones asserts that it restricted and penalized student choices in relation to their clothing or manifestation of religious symbols, which potentially conflicts with the right to freedom of religious expression. As such, under this legislation:

> Muslim girls wearing the headscarf may be expelled from school whether or not they have engaged in political or proselytizing activities, disrupted teaching or disturbed public order.
>
> (ibid.: 16)

The right to adapt school uniform to reflect Islamic principles is one of the attractions for parents in choosing Muslim schools (Parker-Jenkins, 2002), although today most community schools in England provide for adaptation of school dress for both genders from a Muslim background and other faith groups.

Islamic values of *purdah* (screen or veil) and protecting Muslim women from contact with men from outside their family are also related to *izzet* or family honour, which some Muslims see as being borne by female family members (Shaw, 1988; Peach, 2005). This is a shared concern within Muslim school communities, and the issue of gender was an important consideration in our case study schools (Parker-Jenkins, 2008), especially those at secondary level. In some cases, the school was chosen because it could be relied upon to provide a high level of security, especially where female pupils were concerned. This was noted as follows:

> ... to keep a safe environment; all females safe and secure. If you get one of the prospectuses you will see that it is all-female education within a secure environment.
>
> (Headteacher, independent Muslim girls' secondary school)

This line of thought extended to the employment of staff: 'Whenever an advert goes in the paper [it] always states that it is a genuine reason why it is only women applicants' (ibid.). (There are a variety of ways in which this is provided: single sex schools, separate floors within the same institution, or separate school buildings.) Visitors to the school are carefully monitored:

> ... our literacy co-ordinators were all male and I did say at a meeting that they can't come into the school and if Ofsted inspectors visited the school, men were not welcome: when we had an Ofsted [inspection] three years ago it was all women.
>
> (ibid.)

Beyond compulsory schooling, issues of personal dress and behaviour consistent with Islamic principles also have significance. A Muslim student in the UK might later, for example at university, experience more mixing, but as Gilby *et al.* (2011) suggest, although many Muslim students have friends who are not Muslim, some barriers to further mixing exist on university campuses; for example, the focus of many student social activities is around alcohol (which Muslims students must avoid), and Muslim students tend to study only a certain range of subjects.

Having provided a brief overview of Muslim schools in England and the development of an institutional ethos based on Islamic considerations, we look now at the issue of diversity within this category of schools.

Diversity within Muslim schools

Diversity within Muslim schools is often overlooked. There can be multiple dialects, ethnic backgrounds, and nationalities in one single school that reflect the sectarian, ethnic, linguistic, and socio-economic distinctions among Muslim communities. The range of types of schools in the UK is also relevant: there are VA, academy, mosque schools, supplementary schools, *madrassahs*, community schools with a majority of Muslim pupils, *Darul Uloom* schools providing training for future imams and religious leaders, and Muslim schools affiliated to AMS UK.

Within each of these different types of schools are communities representative of different cultural groups and identities. We signalled the overlapping factors in ascribing identity in the Introduction. If we deconstruct the concept of personal identity further we can describe it in a number of ways, including dual, multiple, layered, and gendered characteristics. Linguistic, 'racial', and religious aspects may combine, as well as national and sectarian considerations. Importantly, identity is not fixed but rather dynamic and situational. This is particularly true for children who may have to navigate the cultural identity of the home and the school ethos, to reflect and replicate the values of home life (Hewer, 2001). Halstead (2004) describes Muslim education in terms of (i) aiding individual development;

(ii) increasing understanding of society and its social and moral rules; and (iii) transmitting knowledge, although of course such an analysis is by no means exclusive to Islamic thinking. The complexity of personal identities is captured by a Muslim student in a study by Richardson and Wood:

> I could view myself as a member of the following communities depending on the context and in no particular order: Black, Asian, Azad Kashmiri, Mirpuri, Jat, Marilail, Kungriwaley, Pakistani, English, British, Yorkshireman, from Bradford Moor. Any attempt to define me as only one of these would be meaningless.
> (2004: 4)

These descriptors help explain a person's complex sense of identity and in many instances the different facets of that identity may overlap, be combined, or vary according to the situation or the age of the individual. Shain found in her study of Muslim teenage boys that 'collective identities were built on self definitions as Muslim first' (2011: 77). This was not, however, a fixed identity, for 'the construction of a collective Muslim identity [was] a strategic response to the racialized and stigmatized status of being a Muslim in school' (ibid.).

Having provided brief discussion of Muslim schooling in England and the diversity within the Muslim community, we look next at the experience of engagement and hostility from the wider community. As in the previous chapter on Jewish-based education in England, we draw on data from our case study to help inform this discussion on diversity. Within the Muslim schools in our research, selection was based on institutions providing an Islamic ethos that ranged from orthodox to more liberal in terms of the interpretation of religious texts, willingness to engage with the National Curriculum, and being prepared to provide knowledge of faiths other than Islam. All five schools were Sunni in nature due to the absence of access to those based on a Shia tradition at the time of the study. Selected with the help of AMS UK, the sample did not include *Darul Uloom* or Deobandi school communities, which, as we signalled earlier, have a particular focus on training future imams and religious leaders. Nor did the case study include Muslim seminaries or boarding schools, which were outside of the scope of our study due to difficulty of access (Gilliat-Ray, 2011).

Children in the Muslim schools in our study were predominantly second or third-generation British Muslims from a diversity of backgrounds, for example Pakistani, Bangladeshi, and Middle Eastern. Through interviews and focus groups, we elicited from the five Muslim schools their views on the nature of 'community', cultural sustainability, links outside of their own school community, and experiences of hostility and Islamophobia. The understandings of Islamic principles and community engagement are different among Muslim schools in terms of reaching out to the wider community. We need, therefore, to be nuanced in any discussion of Muslim faith schools, as with others based on religious ethos, in relation to community engagement, and to recognize the complexity and layers of meaning of this activity.

Our case study explored: the needs of Muslim students including proximity to family; admissions policy; access to religious education; resources adapted to a Muslim ethos; levels of engagement and mixing between Muslim students and other students; and levels of cohesion imbued in the curriculum and school ethos. The extent to which students perceive their institution to be one in which students from different backgrounds get on well together and have opportunities to learn about cultural difference also formed part of the discussion. Geographically, these Muslim schools were situated in London, the Midlands, and the north of England and formed part of the provision of Muslim education in England, each operating as part of a wider Muslim community. The majority had an open admissions policy to include non-Muslim pupils.

Concepts of community

The concept of *ummah* is defined as a universal Muslim community of believers throughout the world, crossing all barriers of caste, colour, race, nationality, and territory. Identifying with the *ummah*, including the Sunni and Shia communities, is an element of building internal concepts and a practice of community. The term 'community' in general is contested; it is multiple and contextual in terms of space and scale, and influenced by normative values (Canuto and Yaeger, 2000). Although huge differences exist among Muslims, as we noted earlier, the concept of one universal community (Hulmes, 1989: 32) is significant. Within Islam, the concept of the *ummah* means that differences in 'customs and conventions of different regions give way to the importance of unity and shared practice' (Ashraf, 1993: 3). Further, the preservation and health of the *ummah* are considered an important aspect of the faith (Hulmes, 1989; Sarwar, 1992). As such, Muslim families may perceive their life predominantly within this concept of community, rather than as an independent family or as part of a non-Islamic community.

Despite the common criticism that faith schools are ghettoized or operating in communities of self-imposed segregation, there are a diversity of responses to 'engagement' shown in both the formal and informal curriculum. We found in our case study that the cultural focus in the 'hidden curriculum' – that is, the unofficial and unwritten values, attitudes, and perspectives (Lawton, 1980; Giroux and Purpel, 1983) – forms part of a school's *raison d'etre*, bridging the religious notions of what cohesion means and, for example, exploring Islamic concepts of citizenship. Interestingly, our research revealed parents expressing interest in having more inter-faith events and setting their own boundaries within the home, even when this conflicted with the boundaries set by the school.

In terms of engaging with the wider community, we found examples of good practice and possible ways forward. These schools' engagement took the form of inter-school visits, interfaith religious festivals, charity donations beyond Islamic communities and based on student choice, and volunteer work/visits within and beyond their own faith group. Some schools linked, internationally, again outside of their faith, and a consortium of Muslim schools shared festival and theme-based activities. We return to the issue of community engagement in more detail in the next chapter.

Being part of a group is a key characteristic of Muslim communities. This strongly emerges in the ethos of creating a shared identity within a school. It is hostility from the wider community that can be the real threat to community engagement, and one that has not been sufficiently recognized in the literature. If left unchecked it could produce the very response from faith schools that the critics of faith schools see them making – namely a defensive posture and self-segregation (Berkeley and Sevita, 2008). Our case study revealed one overarching theme emerging from the data: namely, fear, whether founded or not. There was the fear felt by parents about their children being bullied in state comprehensive schools because of their origin. Similarly, fear of moral permissiveness in these schools was cited, particularly by respondents in the Muslim schools with reference to adolescent girls. Importantly, parents and teachers in both faith communities expressed concern about their children losing their religion and group identity if they were to be educated in non-faith schools.

Fear of the wider community can be experienced by any school based on religious or philosophical difference, but Muslim schools in England and elsewhere are cognizant of the possibility of hostility, which may take the form of Islamophobia and which causes a particular response in terms of keeping their community safe.

Islamophobia and issues of security

The choice of schooling for the purposes of sustaining cultural identity is a key theme, especially among minority ethnic groups, but in the case of

Muslim schools they can be magnets for intolerance. In debates around multiculturalism, Muslims, and Muslim communities in particular, have been singled out for criticism. For example, Baroness Valerie Amos announced when launching the Labour Party's debate on community cohesion in 2006 that there were in the UK 'suicide bombers with Yorkshire accents' (Labour Party conference, 26 September 2006). She added that 'our challenge is to engage with and encourage the debate within the Muslim community' (ibid.). Finney and Simpson maintain that 'she clearly signalled that the community cohesion agenda extends into national security' (2009: 108). In a clear nod to Muslim schools, the Department for Innovation, Universities and Skills (2008) stated that extreme violence in the name of Islam was more likely to be embraced by Muslims who socialize, live, and study together in isolation from mainstream society.

The community cohesion agenda was followed by a new counter-terrorism strategy, mapping regions across the country that were perceived as having the potential to nurture extremists and supporters for Al-Qaeda (Dodd, 2010). Haw cautions about 'the potential hazards of creating resistant identities' (2009: 376) as a result of government policy which targets Muslims and Muslim communities in general as a threat to cohesion and security. This is the backdrop shared by Muslim schools in England today, and our case study unearthed a sense of hostility among Muslims because of criticism targeted at their community specifically (Parker-Jenkins, 2008). This impacted on their daily lives and their school community, and linked with their desire to keep students safe outside of school, as captured by this comment:

> The head of science took a group out last summer and she waited until all the other schools went on holiday and she took a residential group. In the past we went down to London to see a play but because of the bombing (we went a week before the bombings) the Governors have put a stop to that.
>
> (Headteacher, Muslim VA school)

Further, this same interviewee observed that 'since the bombings [2005] we have had to take them in a minibus where before we may have caught the train' (ibid.). When asked about the kind of security issues they might be afraid of, this Muslim headteacher reported: 'I think that it is looking at people who are obviously Islamic and maybe being … suspicious'.

We wanted to know if the chaperoning was because of Islamophobic fears or because they were girls, to which she responded:

Possibly both, I think it might be a bit strong [to say] Islamophobic, but it could be, it's just a security thing, you have to have a certain amount of teachers to students.

(ibid.)

This is in keeping with government guidelines for all schools (DfE, 2014), but we think a higher level of care was being carried out in the Muslim schools regarding pupil safety. They were operating at the level of general safety and security, with the fear of potential Islamophobic responses from the external community.

Muir *et al.* (2004) suggest that it is more apt to speak of 'Islamophobias' rather than about a single phenomenon. In the same sentiment, Maussen (2006, as cited by Allen, 2007) stated that the term 'Islamophobia' groups together different forms of discourse, speech, and acts, by suggesting that they all emanate from an identical ideological core. This is what Allen (2007) refers to as an irrational fear of Islam. Writers in Ireland (Carr and Haynes, 2013) and in Australia (Dunn *et al.*, 2007) describe Islamophobia as racialization based around religion and religious identity. Further, the hostility is experienced worldwide, according to Kumar (2012), associating Muslims with irrationality, misogyny, propensities toward violence, and an inability to democratically govern themselves.

There is, according to Allen (2010), a lack of clarity around the term 'Islamophobia'. Weller (2011) finds that most normative definitions of Islamophobia are limited in their scope and fail to take into account the dimensions of hostility that the term denotes. Islamophobia can be both a subjective and objective term and must take into account the nuanced differences between religious, racial, and ethnic discrimination. The tendency to reduce these differences to mere semantics has caused uneasiness with the discourse surrounding Islamophobia. To better explain these numerous dimensions of hostility, Weller (2011) uses the German term *Fremdenfeindlichkeit* (which roughly translates as 'animosity toward strangers'). This term reflects a visceral animosity that is rooted in history, culture, and consciousness. We adopted the broad definition provided by the Runnymede Trust, as signalled at the outset in this book. In this latter definition, the concept is 'unfounded hostility toward Islam, and therefore, fear or dislike of all or most Muslims' (Runnymede Trust, 1997: 1; Runnymede Trust, 2007), and as such we were looking in part at evidence of hostility experienced by stakeholders in our case study schools.

Significantly, anti-Muslim hostility is not a new phenomenon, as documented by Said (2003) and Kumar (2012). From their study of anti-Muslim racism, Carr and Haynes state that:

> Muslim identities and symbols of Islam are frequently presented as synonymous with terrorism, fundamentalism, repression of women and extremism.
>
> (2013: 4)

We noted this earlier with reference to government policy in the last decade. Further, despite generational and shifting cultural differences:

> Muslims ... experience a unique and pernicious form of racist activity with attendant hostility and discrimination that targets people on the basis of their Muslimness.
>
> (ibid.)

Some authors further contend that legislation protecting Muslims from discrimination in the workplace lags behind that of other groups (c.f. Modood, 2005a; Anwar, 2005). Hostility toward Muslim faith schools, in particular, undermines efforts to develop relationships, build trust, and encourage activities that increase engagement and foster a community of learning. In one Muslim school in our case study – a primary school in the Midlands – the principal argued:

> Kids have to live and work in a society which they have to know something about. Just celebrating each other's festivals is a very facile approach – it doesn't teach respect. The kids who throw stones at me or spit at me in the street have been through a multicultural education and probably their parents have – you could say the educational system has failed them.
>
> (Principal, Muslim independent school)

The issues of hostility and security are linked in informing how the school communities saw themselves and responded in keeping safe from threats from the wider community. Safeguarding the faith school community concerned the following: levels of security within the schools; employing security officers; installing CCTV cameras inside and outside the school; maintaining parental involvement; and extending approaches to e-security via ICT. The need for safety from the 'outside' community/ies concerns all schools, but for those in our case study, their experiences meant they were obliged to take this very seriously. It is not the case, however, that only

Jewish and Muslim schools may be vulnerable, as noted in the work of Weller (2011).

As highlighted earlier in the chapter, one of the things we wanted to discover was how Muslim schools deal with Islamophobia. It was difficult to get an exact sense of this. For example, some of the Muslim girls in our case study schools said they were used to being called a 'Paki' when they went to town, and they did not immediately separate their religious and ethnic identity. A number of writers such as Shain (2011) and Devine (2011) have highlighted the significance of race, ethnicity, and identity in school children and the negative treatment they have experienced. School management in our study saw the issue more in terms of protecting community members who, as well as attracting attention because of their race or ethnicity, may also dress visibly differently, which brings issues of its own:

> We actually are responsible for developing a procedure for dealing with these issues. ... You have seen me, someone who is different, and we say that this [hostility] is not acceptable and we have got procedures to deal with it. If it is directed to me I have to report it to my manager and they have to take action, if you can take action.
>
> (School governor, Muslim VA secondary school)

When asked if they felt there was a sense of 'strength in numbers' which provides protection, one female teacher explained:

> It depends on what area you are [in], if you were in this area then yes. If you moved away slightly, you are in a minority, if you were in town for example and you were shopping and people see you alone then people will have a go at you.
>
> (Teacher, independent Muslim primary school)

In terms of whether this was associated with perceptions of terrorism, she contended that the hostility was related to a number of issues such as anti-Muslim fears since 9/11. It is noteworthy that, among Muslims respondents, hostility from the outside community was associated with a perception of lack of acceptance:

> Those people who have tried to become part of the community have been rejected. ... at the moment we don't think we have been accepted by the majority of the community because we are always being undermined and if you are being undermined you have to associate with something else ... Muslims feel under

> quite a lot of pressure … say today news came on and there is an explosion on a bus in London … it could be a petrol tank exploded but it seems that the fault only lies with Muslims and it doesn't lie with anything else, we are the cause for everything.
>
> (ibid.)

This view is reflected in the work of Modood (2005) in terms of a lack of belonging expressed by immigrants despite long-term residency in the UK. It may also be that there is pressure on minority groups to integrate, which may also cause people to affiliate with their ethnic group. However, we believe that it is this perception and experience of being unwelcome, rather than an attachment to their country of origin, which diminishes a sense of belonging in British society. For both Jews and Muslims, family ties and the presence of people with similar religious and ethnic backgrounds were seen as an important reason for moving to, and valuing, the locality in which they lived and from which they chose their school. Research shows that both migrants and established Muslim residents derive a sense of security from the presence of people sharing their religion, ethnicity, or country of origin in their locality (Jayaweera and Choudhury, 2008).

The pupil focus groups in our case study clearly showed that the experience of Islamophobia from the wider community made their school feel like a safe haven. For example, Muslim girls said that outside school they had had their *hijabs* or headscarves pulled off, accompanied by verbal abuse such as 'you f'ing Muslim'. This generated a sense of a 'them-and-us' culture, as a result of which safety rested within the school and the Muslim community.

All schools in the UK have to be vigilant to potential attacks, and there is evidence of an increase in violence in British schools, as in the USA (Larkin, 2007) and in Europe (*The Independent*, 2007). However, Muslim schools are particularly vulnerable to hostility that can be defined as Islamophobia (Runnymede Trust, 2007). For example, in our case study, a female Muslim teacher working in a girls' secondary school in the North of England stated:

> Here there are many, many Sikh women that have been attacked because people assume they are Muslim. I don't know what your religion is, but if you went out in this dress, people would assume that you are Muslim just because you have a headscarf on and they would have a go at you.
>
> (Teacher, VA Muslim girls' secondary school)

She added, with reference to community relations:

> Certainly xenophobia has increased since 9/11… and here at the moment there are two issues, one is Palestine and Israel … and then there is Afghanistan, Iraq, and America and so forth, and that is a separate issue. But it seems that they have joined the two together and they are using the word 'terrorist' for everything and anything.
>
> (ibid.)

This was further illustrated with reference to the role of some sections of the media:

> For example, if I go tonight and burn a shop and someone knew it was me, in the newspaper it would more than likely say a 'Muslim terrorist'. If a non-Muslim, they would say it was an arson attack. Only last week, there was a man who said he had a rucksack with a bomb in it, but he was white, so what the police did was shoot him with rubber bullets … this [other] guy was walking up and down and he looked like an Asian. If he had a beard and he actually said he had explosives in his bag they would have used live bullets on him … that is Islamophobia.
>
> (ibid.)

Muslim schools in particular have been singled out for criticism as symbols of fundamentalism and as a rallying point for violence (Dawkins, 2001; Toynbee, 2001; British Humanist Association, 2002; Berkeley and Sevita, 2008). Writers such as Halstead and McLaughlin (2005) have forcefully challenged this, stating that there has been no evidence to support such accusations – a debate we return to in the final chapter of the book.

Within our case study there was no consistency in views surrounding hostility, with many parents saying it was inevitable that their children would face these issues in their lives. Importantly, we found that children were more vulnerable than adults to incidents of Islamophobia, as in the cases of anti-Semitism discussed in Chapter 3. Incidents went unreported or stayed between children and parents. Despite these omissions or differences in perception, we found evidence of mechanisms having been put in place within the school to ensure security and protection from wider society. Issues of safety impact on the experience of schooling for both Jewish and Muslim children, and these matters, rather than notions of religious identity, may underpin 'choice' in the school context. The sense of insecurity that many parents feel has led them to choose religious schools as safe havens from racism (Parker-Jenkins, 2002; Hewer, 2001).

In terms of disengagement or self-segregation, there is a fear of assimilation (versus integration) into British society (Modood, 2013; Triandafyllidou, 2012), and this is seen as one of the main factors preventing minority groups from integrating fully with the host society:

> ... here we are a community; we are all together in the same situation, so it just builds up your self-esteem. Being in this society ... you are not anything ... here we are together ... and we don't have to face anything.
>
> (Muslim students' focus group)

The schools in our case study were operating on a number of levels – religious, cultural, and academic – in response to parental choice and expectations. There was a marked difference between primary and secondary schools in that as soon as children were able to travel to school by themselves they were more vulnerable to hostility from others in the form of Islamophobic bullying and anti-Semitic verbal assaults. For example, Muslim girls reported being targeted by members of the wider community in the form of abuse due to physical appearance and wearing the *hijab*. Our research project uncovered, at both primary and secondary level, very concerning incidents of bullying and name-calling outside of the school and within the pupils' recreation time, or during travel to and from school or to the mosque for prayer.

Religious groups can be particularly vulnerable to hostility as a result of choice of dress, as described by this Muslim student:

> ... I was outside of [another city] and we were coming back [home] and we were going past a pub, obviously I had my *hijab* on and I was sitting in the back of the car with my dad and it was summer so the windows were down, and they said 'Aye Pakis go back home', it was really offensive but we couldn't exactly do anything, so my dad said just ignore it so we just went on ... it is quite common.
>
> (Student, Muslim girls' VA secondary school)

As we noted earlier, the wearing of the *hijab* is characteristic of most Muslim schools, as in our case study. The *hijab* is frequently associated with Muslims, based on Islamic identity, and closely connected to both an individual and group sense of identity (Jackson and Doerschler, 2012;

Muslim schools and concepts of community

Runnymede Trust, 2007). Further, in Muslim communities in the West, the right for female Muslims to wear the *hijab* exists as an important aspect of everyday life. Modood (1998) advocates for differences to be recognized in the public domain as part of 'ethnic assertiveness' and a moving away from the discourse of cultural assimilation:

> Equality is not having to hide or apologize for one's origins, family or community but expecting others to respect them and adapt public attitudes ... so the heritage they represent is encouraged rather than contemptuously expected to wither away.
>
> (Modood, 1998: 213)

As such, the obligation or burden of change is not expected to be one-way, as echoed in the work of Finney and Simpson (2009).

In the backlash against cultural or religious diversity alluded to earlier, Muslim schools and communities have become more exposed to public scrutiny (Werbner, 2009) and a perceived threat to social cohesion in Britain ('Lessons in Hate and Violence', 2011). Respondents in the Muslim schools in our research noted the perception that some of the broader community feared them and they were seen as linked to extremism, radicalism, and terrorism. By 'the broader community', they generally meant people who were not Muslim. Interestingly, within both Jewish and Muslim school communities they also referred to members within the same broad religious group who shared very different views. For example, one Muslim school described itself as 'orthodox' and acknowledged that other Muslim schools in the region distanced themselves and saw this institution as practising a more rigid interpretation of Islamic principles that placed more restrictions on the curriculum and engagement with the non-Muslim community. Similarly, within both the Jewish and Muslim school communities there were differing opinions about each other. On the one hand, some sought assistance to support inter-faith dialogue for their pupils through linking with schools outside of their faith. This was partly informed by the legal obligation on schools at this time to demonstrate their role in promoting community cohesion under the prevailing legislation (Education and Inspections Act, 2006; DCSF, 2007a). On the other hand, others chose not to associate with other religious schools, or those within their own faith whom they described as 'too liberal' or 'too orthodox', and instead focused on developing their own ethos. We discuss patterns and skills around engagement in the next chapter.

Summary

This chapter discussed Muslim education in England, highlighting differences within Muslim schools, issues of gender, and concepts of community. The significance of community and the *ummah* were discussed, including how the concept of 'community' has particular meaning for Muslims. Evidence from our case study was used to highlight the experience of hostility from the wider community, issues of security, and instances of Islamophobia. The experiences and challenges captured in our case study research (Parker-Jenkins, 2008) were explored and the challenges for the external community in recognizing and accepting cultural difference were also highlighted. The concept of engagement at a broader level and the skills needed to equip children to lead in the twenty-first century form the basis of the next chapter.

Chapter 5
Skills for engagement

> We need ... the first truly global generation; a generation of individuals rooted in their own cultures but open to the world and confident of their ability to shape it.
>
> (Barber *et al.*, 2012: 10)

Introduction

So far we have looked at the antagonism from the wider community experienced by some faith schools in Britain due to perceptions of self-segregation. We will now address what schools can do practically to promote positive relations and define and refine the skills needed to do so. Importantly, we look here at what *all* schools can do, rather than assuming that responsibility rests only or predominantly with faith schools. We propose here an alternative framework for engagement within wider discussions around twenty-first-century skills. To explore these points in detail, the discussion in this chapter focuses on:

- the concept of community engagement;
- a framework for skills for engagement;
- defining and assessing twenty-first-century skills;
- and implications for policy and practice.

Toward community engagement

Drawing on our case study, we define the term 'engagement' as the practice of mixing and working with/alongside others, for example family members, other schools, the police force, and so on. This can extend to the ability or willingness of different communities to live alongside and with other communities. By identifying and employing different levels of community engagement and providing a framework, schools can affirm and support an environment of 'reaching out' that goes beyond 'tokenism' and provides a truly twenty-first-century pedagogy. This chapter reflects the emphasis placed on building a twenty-first-century education system in which schools are at the heart of their local communities (DCSF, 2007a). To accomplish this, we look to other models that can help prepare children with twenty-first-century skills and highlight implications for policy and practice in schools.

A growing body of literature supports the assertion that in order to effectively provide twenty-first-century learning skills, a school should be permeable and able to learn and improve through full engagement with the local community. It is with this permeability that the interior community ethos of a school can effectively promote engagement, which in turn facilitates the acquisition of twenty-first-century skills.

Our model of engagement extends to all stakeholders and is best operationalized at a number of levels within and beyond the faith grouping. As West-Burnham *et al.* state:

> Guiding learning in the community, when the goals of equity, wellness and achievement are of equal importance, requires that all stakeholders build relationships with each other that increase educational opportunity and success, first for children and youths and then for all members of the community.
>
> (2007: 60)

Schools, and especially faith schools, belong to communities – they do not stand alone. In an atmosphere of trust, schools can be seen and view themselves as public spaces. This can encourage connection and in turn promote engagement and interaction within and beyond the school communities. Schools must engage in order to help young people achieve their full potential as adults and to develop a range of skills and knowledge. Consequently, in addition to this proposed model of 'community engagement', we also look at other models that schools could consider in preparing children for life in the twenty-first century.

First, however, we must consider and summarize why community engagement is important at all. Furbey *et al.* (2006) argue that engagement: (i) permits the sharing of people's associations with one another; (ii) provides a supportive context for relationships and associations; (iii) inspires trust and confidence; and (iv) in a school setting, creates a context in which schools can act developmentally and strategically. More simply put, community engagement permits faith communities, and by extension faith schools, to act as hubs for bringing people together, thereby engendering trust. In the next sections, we will examine how trust relates to community engagement, and provide a proposed framework for the conceptualization of it in the context of twenty-first-century learning.

An important aspect of this discussion is the issue of trust between different groups. Trust is both a cause and consequence of community engagement. When networks are maintained and people develop a common understanding, trust emerges. Trust is nurtured through relationships, through information, and through knowledge. The 'trust loop' looks something like this:

- Schools gather *information* about their local community: the history, geography, and key socio-economic factors.
- That information is then turned into *knowledge* and *understanding* – that includes an appreciation of the challenges, riches, and complexities of daily life.
- Knowledge and understanding become the bedrock for building *mutuality* – a shared affinity and allegiance between schools and communities about the education needs of young people.

Our research into the practices of community cohesion in UK schools challenged the assumption that little engagement is taking place among faith schools. The study determined that all the case study schools (both those receiving government funding under VA arrangements and independent schools) had some good strategies in place that reflected various levels of engagement. All of the schools we studied demonstrated degrees of engagement with the community at local, national, and international levels on the basis of their own religious and political agendas.

There is active awareness of responsible citizenship and charitable deeds within both the Jewish and Muslim cultures, based around the concept of doing the right thing and behaving well (Miller, 2011). The Jewish precepts of *tikkun olam* and *tzedakah* incorporate participating in society with courtesy and respect, social justice, and charity. For Muslims, one of the five basic duties, known as the 'Five Pillars of Islam', is *zakah* or 'welfare contribution', which provides the opportunity for contributing to society in a number of ways (Sarwar, 1992: 41). *Tikkun olam*, *tzedakah*, and *zakah* are expressed through charity and social action within and beyond one's own faith group. This was evidenced by the chosen charities of pupils in one Jewish secondary school: 'one British-based Jewish charity, one Israel-based Jewish charity, one non-Jewish, and one African'. Similarly, a Muslim school supported a range of charities, including British, Palestinian, and non-Muslim charities. These altruistic practices can be called upon to facilitate the positive force of community engagement in the context of religious hostility. For example, in a focus group conducted with students at a Muslim VA school it was observed:

> After the riots … they had different people from religions and different backgrounds come together to communicate and get to

> know things about each other's cultures … so you don't have the barrier or end up hating each other.
>
> (Muslim girls' focus group, VA secondary school)

It is fortunate that we need not rely on the aftermath of hostilities to create learning environments conducive to bonding and bridging, for we found that in order to promote children's understanding of the wider community both Jewish and Muslim schools were involved in a variety of different projects. Within the Jewish schools, one teacher in a pluralist school reported that their engagement stretches from links to the local neighbourhood to the global 'and everything in between, both Jewish and non-Jewish'. Similarly, a governor of a modern orthodox Jewish school said they were involved in every aspect and at every level of their community, and their children visited local churches. Visiting and connecting or twinning with different schools, particularly those of a different faith, was an approach used by most of the schools in our study. The role of *chessed* (wisdom) activities, seen to be community service, active citizenship, and social cohesion are deeply important to schools, as marked out in recent Pikuach (Jewish religious school inspection) reports (Miller, 2011). Similarly, a consortium of Jewish schools organized 'Multicultural Weeks' whereby individual schools prepared work around a theme within cultural pluralism, and this was shared among others: for example, Chinese, Indian, and African-Caribbean weeks (Parker-Jenkins and Glenn, 2011). The Internet and electronic communication were also used, with adult guidance, connecting children of different religious backgrounds.

Reaching out to the wider community was perceived as highly important by one Jewish teacher, as 'a lot of children that go to Jewish schools … don't have a lot of contact with people in the wider world'. One approach was described by the headteacher of a modern orthodox Jewish VA primary school in our study:

> There is a school across the park and we have been to it on several occasions to do assemblies on Hanukah and the Passover. They have been here as well for Divali and Eid. We also did a project on Judaism for a non-Jewish audience.
>
> (Headteacher, modern orthodox VA primary school)

This inclusive and dialogue-driven process is about a commitment to creating dynamic, two-way partnerships and seeking and finding common ground. Community engagement brings the community into schools and moves out from the school into the community. Initiatives designed to bring children

Skills for engagement

together from different schools should be structured around cooperation and engagement. It is in this shared space of common ground that real, committed, and measurable community engagement can occur.

A framework for skills of engagement

The schools in our case study (Parker-Jenkins, 2008) were all involved in charitable events and curricular initiatives that linked them to activities in both Jewish and Muslim communities, and some reached beyond those faith communities. Dyson and Gallannaugh (2008) have also conducted work on community engagement, suggesting that the concept can be explained in a number of ways. Gaine (2005) and Carroll (2003) have conceptualized it on four levels: fully engaged, vicariously engaged, semi-engaged, and under-engaged. Building on this literature and informed by our case study, we propose another model of engagement for schools. This is based on the spectrum in Figure 1, which demonstrates the different levels of engagement:

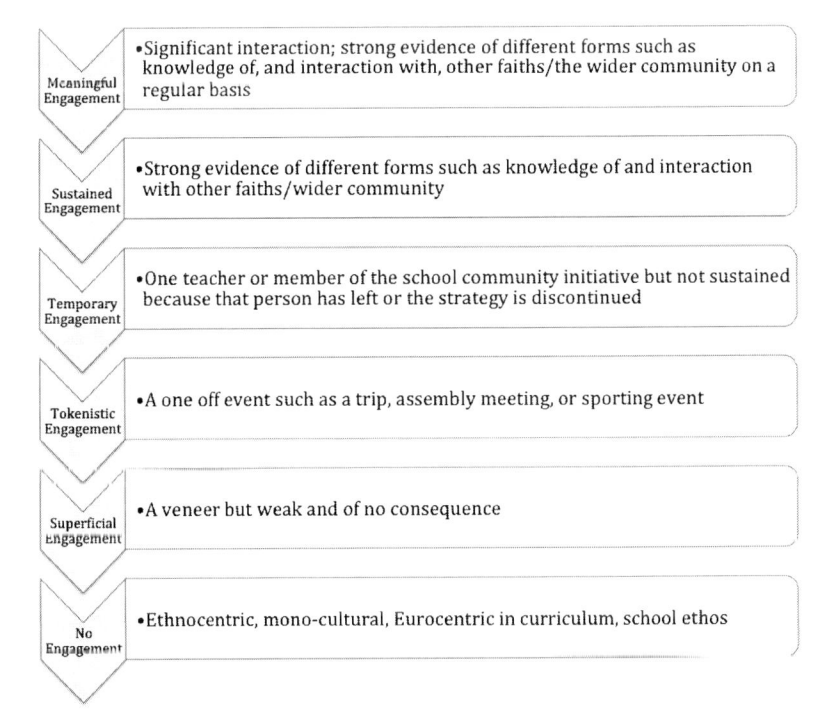

Meaningful Engagement	Significant interaction; strong evidence of different forms such as knowledge of, and interaction with, other faiths/the wider community on a regular basis
Sustained Engagement	Strong evidence of different forms such as knowledge of and interaction with other faiths/wider community
Temporary Engagement	One teacher or member of the school community initiative but not sustained because that person has left or the strategy is discontinued
Tokenistic Engagement	A one off event such as a trip, assembly meeting, or sporting event
Superficial Engagement	A veneer but weak and of no consequence
No Engagement	Ethnocentric, mono-cultural, Eurocentric in curriculum, school ethos

Figure 1: A framework for community engagement (adapted from Parker-Jenkins and Glenn, 2011)

Applying the framework in Figure 1, Miller (2011) described the engagement levels in Jewish schools as follows:

> Jewish schools in the UK engage the wider community at various levels of intensity between categories ... In the current political climate, there is no possibility for State schools of any kind in Britain to be at level six, that is, having no contact with others within and beyond the school community. Even those Jewish schools who feel strongly that they want to have as little as possible to do with the wider community show some weak engagement with people beyond the school gates. Conversely, very few Jewish schools exhibit 'significant interaction', although this may be more about having insufficient time and resources than a lack of interest or desire.
>
> (Miller, 2011: 36)

It is also important to note that community schools of no religious affiliation should seek opportunities for pupils to mix and develop their own understanding and valuing of cultural diversity beyond their school community; parents, not just teachers or pupils, need to be brought on board in this initiative. Schools need to work hard to gain the support of parents, some of whom, we found from our case study, have chosen a faith school for their children precisely because they do not want them to mix with children of other backgrounds.

We suggest that the application of the framework described in Figure 1 is best achieved by incorporating it into a school development plan, identifying what has already been achieved, setting out school priorities, establishing values, and developing the curriculum. It should be possible for schools to map the different levels of awareness and commitment to action by different stakeholders within the school. This would avoid activities of engagement being carried out by only one group, such as teachers, and would require pupils and parents to have relevant opportunities. There is also evidence of 'associational engagement' (Varshney, 2002) with more formal political and civic interaction. For example, we found in our case study that having connections with groups in Israel or Palestine was considered important for schools, as it also relates to groups within the same religious traditions.

Defining and assessing twenty-first-century skills

The impetus in building twenty-first-century skills lies largely on schools developing a skills-based pedagogy. Under section 78 of the Education Act (2002), schools are seen as locales for the 'physical, mental, social, cultural and moral development' of young people. The debate over whether faith schools provide the adequate development that prepares young people for adulthood and gives them the ability to operate effectively in a multi-ethnic,

Skills for engagement

multi-faith society is filled with both praise and concern, as we noted in Chapter 2. Supporters of faith schools claim they give pupils a strong sense of personal worth and highlight their ability to prepare pupils to be good citizens (Ofsted, 2009). Moreover, schools with a high social capital have a significant advantage, which explains the successes of many faith schools – they have a ready-made sense of community. Effective communities combine the capacity to bond with the ability to bridge (West-Burnham et al., 2007).

However, there are also concerns that a narrow curriculum prevents young people from participating in a pluralistic society outside of their own family and community. Opponents of faith schools maintain that children are raised in a segregated community, unaware of others outside their faith group, and that this can lead to intolerance (Berkeley and Sevita, 2008; Dawkins, 2001). Although Berkeley and Sevita (2008) contend that pupils in faith schools gain valuable communication and collaboration skills as a result of a value-based education and strong ties with the community, this, they suggest, is not enough to prepare young people for living and working in a multi-faith society, because of the limited opportunities for young people to mix with people of different backgrounds.

Faith schools and others will have to grapple with the extent to which they are prepared to facilitate opportunities for their pupils to communicate with their peers from outside of their own community, and how to adequately prepare them for life in the twenty-first century. Their response to these challenges will be based on their school ethos and what might best serve the school community interest, but they must also recognize the importance of providing their pupils with opportunities for meaningful engagement with the wider society. In taking such initiatives further, there are implications for schools in terms of policy and practice.

Within this broad umbrella of what children need for their futures, we suggest twenty-first-century skills models. These models demonstrate that within teaching and learning, practitioners should focus on skill development and how it can infiltrate the curriculum and teaching. The key question is: what skills do children need for the future? We think the approach of twenty-first-century skills has particular value, because there is a good synergy with the area of fostering better relations among different ethnic groups in society. The 'race' debates appear outdated now, and we need to consider how students may have access to better skills development through the curriculum experience in schools. This would require a departure from the more simplistic approach to learning about religious diversity.

In looking at being skilled to lead in the twenty-first century, we need to look at where there is overlap between twenty-first-century skills and the varied approaches that faith schools take. Where do the twenty-first-century models overlap with the aims of faith schools, and others, and what does this overlap look like? How is it assessed? Importantly for our discussion, how does it relate to the framework of community engagement and the integration of community engagement into twenty-first-century learning? We suggest that schools that rank higher on the community engagement continuum are those that help children to develop the skills necessary to understand and engage with issues of tolerance of other communities. This would be a departure from learning at the level of basic knowledge informed by lists of facts. West-Burnham *et al.* (2007) share the concern that we have become too dependent on a pedagogy of memorization. In response to this, Pellegrino and Hilton (2012) propose a process of 'deeper learning', where an individual becomes capable of taking what was learned in one situation and applying it to new situations. Skills must be transportable and transferable – young people should be readily able to transfer skills learned in one situation to another. Deeper learning enables students to transfer learning into the real world and use this knowledge to solve new problems, rather than simply being able to store information or recall facts. This includes 'transferable knowledge', 'content knowledge', and 'procedural knowledge'.

While useful, *knowledge of* other communities by itself is not sufficient; what students also need for the future are *skills*. A number of writers and organizations have been looking into what children need to know in the future beneath the umbrella term 'twenty-first-century skills' (see, for example, Koenig, 2011; Pellegrino and Hilton, 2012; Barber *et al.*, 2012; Suto, 2013). Below, we summarize the salient points of some key models. Pellegrino and Hilton (2012) further illustrate that this blend of content knowledge and related skills should be referred to as 'twenty-first-century competencies' and that twenty-first-century skills and competencies are essential for:

- educational achievement and attainment;
- professional accomplishment;
- health and relationships;
- civic participation.

Young people must be able to thrive, adapt, and develop skills that are deemed critical for success in higher education and the workplace. These skills include:

> … being able to solve complex problems, to think critically about tasks, to effectively communicate with people from a variety of different cultures and using a variety of different techniques, to

work in collaboration with others, to adapt to rapidly changing environments and conditions for performing tasks, to effectively manage one's work, and to acquire new skills and information on one's own.

(Koenig, 2011: 1)

Twenty-first-century skills are of particular importance to faith schools in their ability to build capacity and develop leadership. Levels of social capital have a direct effect on the educational and personal success of a child. Koenig suggests a useful starting point is to ask: what do children need to learn to prepare for a demanding competitive world? He answers:

- cognitive skills – non-routine problem-solving and systems thinking;
- interpersonal skills – social intelligence required for relating to other people;
- intrapersonal skills – adaptability and self-management/self-development.

(Koenig, 2011)

Two frameworks: 'Partnership for twenty-first-century skills' (P-21), and 'Assessment and teaching of twenty-first-century skills' (ATCS21, see Table 2) provide differing but complementary guidance on the key skills necessary for pupils to achieve success in school and in the workplace.

Table 2: Definitions of twenty-first-century skills

P-21		ATCS21
Work creatively with others	Ways of thinking	Creativity & Innovation
Communicate clearly		Critical thinking, problem-solving, decision-making
Collaborate with others		Learning to learn, metacognition
Adapt to change	Ways of working	Communication
Be flexible		Collaboration (teamwork)
Interact effectively with others	Tools for working	Information literacy
Work effectively in teams		ICT literacy
Guide and lead others	Living in the world	Citizenship – local & global
Be responsible to others		Life & career
		Personal & social responsibility

Source: P-21 excerpted from Koenig (2011), ATCS21 from Suto (2013)

A different conceptualization is provided by Florida *et al.* (2005). They state, in what is known as the '3 Ts' model, that we need to develop talent, technology, and tolerance. Again, this is useful to this discussion because it places an emphasis on the issue of 'tolerance', which theoretically was to be achieved through the now-abandoned community cohesion agenda. But what does tolerance mean, how is it enacted, and how can it be assessed? We are suggesting that the answer lies in helping children to develop *the skills* necessary to understand and engage with issues of tolerance of other communities.

Barber *et al.* (2012: 49–50) simplify an approach to preparing for twenty-first-century learning with reference to a helpful formula: 'Well-educated = E (K+T+L)'. Overall, this formula is based on the view that a curriculum that combines knowledge with thinking and leadership underpinned by ethics better prepares young people for life in the twenty-first century (Barber *et al.*, 2012). The K stands for knowledge – meaning 'know how' as well as 'skills such as those related to information technology, taking notes or making a succinct summary' (Barber *et al.*, 2012: 49). The T stands for thinking or thought: 'the evidence shows overwhelmingly that when children are taught to think, and to reflect on how they are thinking as they learn their subjects, their performance significantly improves' (ibid.: 49).

The L in this model stands for leadership, 'in the sense of being able to influence those around you in the family, community, workplace or classroom' (Barber *et al.*, 2012: 50). As such, this model suggests that rather than there being a separate set of classes in 'thinking skills', teachers should be prepared to teach different approaches to thinking through their subjects, developing critical thinking skills to make decisions about key issues or different groups. This is a particularly useful strategy when challenging negative stereotypes and the mythology surrounding particular groups such as Muslim communities (Shain, 2009; Finney and Simpson, 2009). Finally, E stands for ethics, which are informed by the way a school operates, 'the way the teachers and students interact, and the way the school interacts with the communities it serves' (Barber *et al.*, 2012: 51). For this reason, the E in the model lies outside of the bracket.

Implications for education policy and practice

Future education systems will need to innovate and think creatively about what children need to learn: the necessary skills as well as knowledge. The twenty-first-century frameworks we have discussed have implications for the way schools are organized and the role of the teacher. Barber *et al.*

(2012) have written passionately about twenty-first-century skills and 'the oceans of innovation', with a shift from the Atlantic to the Pacific Rim for guidance as to how education can be shaped. There will be implications for schools in terms of how curricular opportunities are provided, for example, with 30-minute or one-hour structures being replaced by half- or whole-day sessions. Suggested approaches are to collapse the routine timetable altogether for two or three days every month or so, in order to break the students into teams and give them a cross-disciplinary task (ibid.). Similarly, the role of the teacher will need to change, becoming that of a facilitator rather than a pedagogue as traditionally understood (ibid.). It is not the case that technology should replace the teacher, but issues of cultural diversity, religion, and belief are particularly important areas that require a skills-based approach, with appropriate learning experiences for children to learn of, and from, each other, and importantly not be threatened by other cultural groups.

All these components are interconnected in the process of twenty-first-century teaching and learning, and the elements represent 'the critical systems necessary to ensure twenty-first-century readiness for every student … [and] to produce a support system that produces twenty-first century outcomes for today's students' (Hattie and Yates, 2011: 49). The curriculum in the Barber *et al.* model is seen as a platform for twenty-first-century skills, distinct from the school systems of the twentieth century that were based on a restrictive curriculum with emphasis on assessment and league tables rather than the needs of the learner (Apple, 2012). To accompany new types of learning, new types of assessment are required. This may be found in the proposed collaborative problem-solving tests for the Programme for International Student Assessment (PISA) in 2015 (OECD, n.d.). Overall, Barber *et al.* (2012) maintain we must be ready for the society of the future, and assert that some of the elements that will drive that change can be predicted.

The discussions here have demonstrated how children can be brought together using technology and learn about different values, beliefs, and lifestyles. Practitioners will also need to involve themselves with this approach, communicating with their peers in different ethnic and cultural communities and using education conferences for policy-makers and educators. Miller *et al.* (2011) note that in education reports commissioned and published by the government and others, there has been a tendency to emphasize policy perspectives rather than classroom practice. As well as a policy gap, there is a practice gap, where schools are left to determine whether they will engage further in good practice, and what possibilities there are whereby pupils can meet each other and communicate at a global level (Miller *et al.*, 2011).

As we have signalled in this chapter, the challenge will be for both teachers and parents to recognize the importance of twenty-first-century skills. This should be supported through teaching practices that create a positive learning community in which students gain knowledge and also develop intrapersonal and interpersonal competencies. Teacher training programmes will need to help teachers develop visions of learning and of how to put knowledge and skills into practice.

Faith schools are an essential part of this equation. 'Faith-based projects and faith buildings are not always what they seem to be to outsiders – they may provide places and spaces where people "negotiate difference" and "transgress" the normal boundaries of interaction' (Furbey *et al.*, 2007: 6). Within a faith-based context, pupils can be taught twenty-first-century skills through school-linking, intercultural programmes, leadership connections across schools, and tutoring between schools. These can lend themselves to deeper and better-embedded aspects of the school curriculum, ethos, and leadership training.

The Tony Blair Faith Foundation provides an example of these initiatives in action. A primary aim of this organization is to recognize the significance of faith and that it can be distorted to fan the flames of extremism. As such, the Foundation 'promotes respect and understanding about the world's religions through education and multi-faith action' (Tony Blair Faith Foundation, n.d.). On a practical level, the Foundation supports and collaborates with initiatives that aim to educate and develop understanding about religion in the modern world. One of the programmes under this Foundation that is particularly relevant to our discussion is Face to Faith (ibid.), a schools programme for 12–17-year-olds. The Face to Faith programme connects students worldwide via a secure website where they interact and 'discuss global issues from a variety of faith and belief perspectives' (ibid.). Specifically, the programme aims:

- to promote cross-cultural understanding, equipping young people with key twenty-first-century skills needed to live in a world of diverse faiths and beliefs
- to provide young people with the knowledge, skills, and competencies needed for meaningful inter and intra-faith dialogue across a range of cultures, containing diverse and often conflicting views, and to give students key mediation and negotiation skills so that they are able to hold meaningful and respectful interfaith discussions.

(Tony Blair Faith Foundation, n.d.)

Summary

Our case study research set out to investigate how Jewish and Muslim faith schools approached concepts of community, and how their strategies aimed to develop cohesion within and beyond their own communities. Given the UK government policy of financial support for faith schools, it is possibly more difficult to avoid new dividing lines or prevent the spiral of separation. In this chapter, we proposed a framework for schools to assess work that is being done within a community engagement approach, which is a more practical and less aspirational approach to the now-abandoned community cohesion strategy. Building on what schools have been doing to help their pupils engage with the wider world, we discussed twenty-first-century skills models with a focus on the skills as well as the knowledge that children need. We also, importantly, examined where there is overlap with the former community cohesion agenda, and discussed what schools might do practically in the classroom to help young people share their religious heritage while contributing to reducing intolerance.

Students need to build the skills and the knowledge base to draw on the social capital from their religious and non-religious communities. As such, we need to consolidate the more readily attainable initiatives of engagement, which for some schools may be at an early stage, and consider more carefully the leadership and teaching strategies that might make further development achievable. More broadly, we also need to consider the wider context and where faith schools fit within a multicultural society. This forms the basis of discussion in the final chapter of this book.

Chapter 6
Conclusion
Where 'reaching' starts and stops

> *Integrating without assimilating ... is a challenge in a wider society.*
> (Miller, 2011: 40)

It is difficult to avoid new dividing lines or prevent the spiral of separation. Legislation has been passed to extend choice in education, which has included schools characterized by religious affiliation and ethos. There has been support for this across the political spectrum, and the expansion of faith-based schooling has become part of the educational landscape. The British government is attempting to balance competing interests between teachers' unions, parental choice, and political agendas while at the same time trying to cohere around a set of values and raise academic results. However, in the policy vacuum left by the movement away from the community cohesion agenda and confusion as to the meaning behind the Big Society initiative, there is a need for better understanding of good practice so as to focus on students gaining the skills necessary to actively participate and lead in the twenty-first century.

This book set out to add nuance to the debates regarding how Jewish and Muslim faith schools approach the concept of community and the various models around wider community engagement. As notions of community are inherent to these two faiths, the school ethos around cultural sustainability and issues concerning Islamophobia and anti-Semitism shed light on the lived experience of those within religious school communities. Further, we looked at how the British government approaches the issues around integration and multiculturalism strategically and how schools endeavour to navigate these policies. To explore these themes, this concluding chapter:

- provides a brief review of the overall discussions and cumulative arguments;
- explores the alleged failure of multiculturalism in Britain;
- considers how faith schools fit within a multicultural society;
- and points to the way forward to support living in a multicultural society.

Conclusion

Overview of discussions

Examining Jewish and Muslim school communities, our case study has been a springboard to explore different arguments about education policy and associated discourses. The variety of ways in which the state has responded to religion and education were discussed in Chapter 1, from the traditional support for faith schools in England and Wales, Northern Ireland, Scotland, and the Netherlands, to the French adoption of a secular policy aiming to separate church and state. Based on the tradition of government recognition and financial support in the UK for faith schools, educational institutions working from a Jewish or Islamic ethos were established in pursuit of equality before the law, developing education reflective of the values of the home. The schools in our research illustrated policy developments in terms of reaching out to other communities, in some instances before the government directives made this obligatory. This is particularly important given the criticisms levelled at faith schools, as highlighted in Chapter 2. Chapters 3 and 4 provided insights into this community engagement and the complexity of multiculturalism in practice. The difficulty of being accepted by the wider community was also discussed, as were the experiences of hostility from the wider community. The failure to acknowledge anti-Semitism and Islamophobia, evidenced in the experiences of Jewish and Muslim communities, suggests that previous policy on community cohesion is flawed, particularly the idealism of government policy and the emphasis on schools being the place where community cohesion could be fostered and demonstrated through school inspections. We critiqued this policy further in Chapter 5 and proposed that the concept of community engagement was a more adaptable solution. This was illustrated by examples of practice from our case-study schools and highlighted in a framework for community engagement that all schools could use.

The clergy in the UK was instrumental in establishing education in the UK, and faith schools – both government-funded and independent – are now an established part of today's education landscape. Of the variety of different religious groups represented, those of a Jewish or Muslim ethos have been vulnerable to prejudice and hostility from the wider community, as experienced in the nineteenth century by Catholic school communities (Grace, 2001). Our study assessed how Jewish and Muslim faith schools responded to this hostility and kept safe. This is particularly important in view of the possibility, suggested by Everett (2012), that a hostile posture of the wider environment, real or perceived, triggers a defensive reaction among minority groups – a reaction characterized by a strict maintenance of group cohesion and heavy policing of members internally.

The impetus to build social capital by engaging with various stakeholders within the wider community should be strengthened to help prepare children for the twenty-first century. The strategy in the community cohesion agenda was for political leadership at the national level to insist that schools assume responsibility to effect change. This was in the context of nebulous government policy, an assessment-led curriculum, and an emphasis on accountability and measurability evidenced in league tables – all of which does not necessarily translate into high-level practice. An emphasis on school practices with an absence of corresponding focus on structural inequalities limits the impact of government initiatives regarding community cohesion. The underperformance of children from minority ethnic backgrounds, particularly of immigrant groups into the second and third generations, is an example of this systemic failure (OECD, 2006).

Devine (2011) states that, as institutions, schools are often at the coal face of experiencing social shifts directly through the changing nature of society, and that 'schools are located contradictorily between safe-guarding the past and what is "known", as well as shaping the future' (Devine, 2011: 153). From a sociological perspective, schools are situated therefore between processes of production and reproduction, 'mediating between diverse forces, often in the context of constrained resources and contrasting local dynamics' (ibid.). This is true of all schools, but is particularly apposite for faith schools, which have been established and supported because of their perpetuation of culture and traditions. As religious communities reach in toward each other to share their spiritual and cultural heritage, they are also expected to reach out and be part of the wider community. Identifying the discourses underpinning the community cohesion and Big Society agendas demonstrates the interplay between societal–structural and group dynamics in the experience of religious communities and the wider society. There are, however, non-funded institutions, such as *madrassahs* and *yeshivas*, in which the wide and varied examples of community engagement may not be evident nor even a part of the hidden or overt curriculum. For all faith schools, however, there is a balance to be achieved between reaching out by making necessary contact with the wider community, and reaching in to develop their own ethos, particularly in the light of multiculturalism, which may be perceived as undermining their religious identity and promoting assimilation.

The failure of multiculturalism in Britain

Along with many other scholars and stakeholders within education, we have raised the point, throughout this book, that the jury is out on whether multiculturalism is failing in the UK. This is in the context of a number of events: the 2001 riots placed the spotlight on 'Britishness', Muslims, and notions of citizenship (Independent Review Team, 2001; Cantle, 2006; Fielding, 2005; Modood, 2010); while the events of 9/11, bombings in London (Husband and Alam, 2011), and the Afghanistan and Iraq invasions (Richardson, 2009) have raised further issues about identity and citizenship. Against this backdrop, schools in the UK have been obliged over the last decade to demonstrate how they are developing community cohesion, and this has formed part of the school inspection protocol. The focus has centred on faith schools that have been criticized for adopting an isolationist stance, with Muslim schools in particular attracting criticism.

Trevor Phillips, former Chair of the Equality and Human Rights Commission (EHRC), has helped lead the debate on multiculturalism in the UK, in suggesting that as a policy it has failed to deliver an 'assimilated society':

> The disastrous doctrine of multiculturalism ... has promoted a lethally divisive culture of separateness, in which minority cultures are held to be equal if not superior to the values and traditions of the indigenous majority.
> (Phillips, 2005, as cited in Finney and Simpson, 2009: 108)

There has been a shift from discourses of multiculturalism to ones of assimilation and to notions of citizenship and integration with a focus on community and social cohesion (Thomas, 2012; Werbner, 2009). Finney and Simpson (2009) see this rhetoric as part of a government and public-induced fear that '"self-segregation" maintains and exacerbates conflict' and that religion rather than race has become the significant aspect of debates (Finney and Simpson, 2009: 92). Further, questions of integration are aimed at what minorities have to do to fit in, imposing the responsibility for this on minority communities. Today, multiculturalism in the UK is associated with fear of fundamentalism, particularly Islamic fundamentalism. As a result, rather less attention is paid to other forms of radicalism and consequently other groups are not highlighted. Policies on community relations and the role of schools in supporting the government agenda on promoting greater cohesion have now reached an impasse.

On the part of government, there is a lack of understanding of identity (Brah, 1996), the concept of multiculturalism (Parekh, 2000, 2002a, 2002b), and why the community cohesion agenda failed to achieve its objectives (Wetherell *et al.*, 2007). Minority groups remain isolated and detached from British society. In part as a result of this, the coalition government in the UK has begun to rethink policy on multiculturalism and integration. Cheong *et al.* (2005: 2) refer to this as 'a return to assimilation'.

The respondents in our case study frequently expressed their concerns over the process of assimilation, and this formed part of the raison d'être in parental choice of a faith school, as discussed earlier. Faith schools are uniquely positioned to address these fear-based notions by means of the community engagement model, thereby reaching the difficult place for societal growth that lies between the fear and distrust of nebulous multicultural ethics and fears of assimilation.

As noted in the Introduction, the new policy was largely informed by the influential Cantle and Ouseley reports which asserted that racial segregation and the institutions maintaining it provide a fertile breeding ground for racial hostility, crime, and radicalization (Independent Review Team, 2001; Ouseley, 2001). These reports put the spotlight on minority faith schools, and particularly those serving the Muslim communities, as possible nurseries of separatism, extremism, and fundamentalism. Alibhai-Brown (2000) and Young (2003) added to the suspicion mounted over faith schools by associating those serving only one community with a dysfunctional multiculturalism that erected group boundaries and essentialized minority cultures.

The New Labour government's policy on community cohesion emphasized common values and an overarching identity, including the view that 'the diversity of people's different backgrounds and circumstances … [should be] appreciated and positively valued' (Home Office, 2004: 5), which is reminiscent of multiculturalism. However, it did not address deprivation, inequality, or exclusion. In contrast, the coalition government that followed assigns only a minimal role to the state in promoting integration and social cohesion. The Secretary of State for Education, Michael Gove, has expressed his intention to sharply reduce the bureaucratic burden on schools, cutting away unnecessary duties, processes, guidance, and requirements (DfE, 2010b: 9).

Multiculturalism as a national policy has been undergoing critique and challenge in the last decade with regard to its ability to foster a harmonious and equitable society. However, the concept is a contested term used broadly to describe a number of overlapping elements. There are three aspects in understanding multiculturalism (Uberoi and Modood, 2009; Meer and Modood, 2009). Firstly, multiculturalism denotes a culturally diverse citizenry, or what may be called a 'multicultural society'. A state can react to this culturally diverse society in different ways, for example by trying to assume a neutral position between various cultural groups without any one of them being privileged over the others. However, the need for a common language and norms to regulate collective affairs often leads to the dominance of one language and cultural tradition. Alternatively, a state can aim to assimilate cultural minorities, making them as indistinguishable from the cultural majority as possible. If assimilation is voluntary, or without state coercion, the approach can be uncontroversial. However, if a policy of assimilation infringes individual freedom and creates or reinforces a hierarchy among different cultural values, there is likely to be resistance, which we noted in our case study.

Secondly, countries such as Canada, Britain, and Australia abandoned policies of assimilation in the 1960s, developing formal and informal policies of multiculturalism. Uberoi and Modood explain that this way of understanding multiculturalism aims to reduce fears about cultural difference and address questions of inequality, exclusion, and disadvantage which cultural minorities may experience in subtle yet significant ways. For example, when the state privileges only one religion or provides an ethnocentric approach to the curriculum, cultural–religious minorities may be excluded and treated unequally. Similarly, if public services are offered only in the language of the dominant group, citizens who are less proficient in that language may be disadvantaged.

Multicultural education in schools and promoting race equality are thus used to reduce fears of cultural difference, while anti-discrimination laws, legal exemptions for minority religious practices, providing public services in different languages, and other measures are used to reduce the inequality, exclusion, and disadvantage. There is also multiculturalism in a third sense, as an ideology or vision for the country that affects how a nation changes and continues to change.

Uberoi and Modood (2009) note that politicians increasingly promote 'Britishness', and, by association, highlight those groups who may have difficulty feeling British and part of mainstream society. In redefining what it is to be British, the government introduced new initiatives, such as citizenship ceremonies, which aim to reflect the national character. Similarly, citizenship education is used in the national curriculum to promote core British values. In light of increasing secularism in society, there are also calls to acknowledge non-religious citizens (British Humanist Association, 2002).

Modood (2009) has raised the possibility of a 'moderate secularist' approach to multiculturalism, one that acknowledges the reality of diverse societies and the existence of not only non-religious but also anti-religious sentiments. The place of religion and secularism in multicultural societies has also been the subject of controversy and negotiation in other multicultural societies, such as France (Modood, 2007), Belgium, the Netherlands, and Germany (Modood and Kastoryano, 2006). The value of moderate secularism, notes Modood (2009), is not just that it serves as a rebuttal to radical secularism, but that it provides a more positive recognition and inclusion of secularism within a multicultural setting.

Another key debate within discourses on multiculturalism has been the positioning of Muslim communities. They are a multicultural group united by a faith dimension of religious beliefs and moral values. Shain (2011) explains that since the 1950s, and even before this, Muslims were seen initially as part of a wider Asian group, challenging social exclusion, poor working and housing conditions, and violent racist attacks. Recent economic, political, and social conditions, however, have brought Islamic identities to the fore. Shain notes the British attempt to 'manage diversity', informed by the government's counter-terrorism initiative, the Prevent Strategy (2006). She highlights the role that education has played in the construction of minority ethnic groups as 'problems' to be contained, arguing that assimilation into a 'superior' British culture has remained a constant theme but becomes more pronounced in periods of economic downturn. Significantly for this discussion, the targets of containment policies have now changed, from African-Caribbeans, predominantly, in the 1970s and 1980s, to Muslims in general. This has been echoed by others, for example by Modood (2003) who states: 'there is an anti-Muslim wind blowing across the European continent' (Modood, 2003: 100). This is noted in the work of Finney and Simpson (2009), who challenge media statements about Muslims, finding in their research that areas with high concentrations of Muslims are no more likely to produce terrorists than other areas. Shain (2011) adds that 'race' has now also been re-coded through ethnicity, community, and/or faith, forming a central reference point in state discourses on minorities.

Expanding the understanding of ethnicity in Britain, Khattab *et al.* (2011) signal the relationship between religion and class. They argue that the class structure of the South-Asian groups is highly ethnicized, in that ethno-religious background and social class are interwoven to such an extent that separating them is challenging, if not impossible. (This overlap or complexity of ethno-religious identification was noted in our case study, discussed in Chapters 3 and 4.) Modood and Dobbernack (2011) suggest that what is needed is a more plural approach to a multicultural community. This involves new understandings about culture, identity, difference, and equality, with a need to reference and acknowledge the place of minorities and difference. They note there has been a major division in the multicultural constituency, and that now is the time to recognize new debates. There are, for example, differences in how non-white Britons conceive of themselves and their positioning, identities, and relationship with society and with others.

Meer and Modood (2009) note that British multiculturalism has allegedly buckled under various Muslim-related pressures. This is signalled in a so-called retreat from the ideology of multiculturalism toward increased governmental emphasis on integration and the now-abandoned social cohesion policy (DfE, 2012a). They challenge this view that British multiculturalism is subject to a wholesale retreat, and suggest instead that it has been, and continues to be, subject to an ongoing critique that is resulting in 'civic re-balancing' (Meer and Modood, 2009: 473), shaped by a more dynamic political multiculturalism. Traditional recognition of cultural 'difference', prejudice reduction, and anti-racism (Troyna and Carrington 1990), with an emphasis on promoting equality of access and opportunity into Britain's self-image, have led to some significant accommodations for certain groups, and Muslim minorities are currently appealing to this tradition as one means of achieving greater inclusion. Lobbying for faith schools based on an Islamic ethos with parity of esteem with other denominational groups in Britain is an example of this activity (Parker-Jenkins, 2002).

Part of the debate about the alleged demise of multiculturalism is the positioning of minority groups. With reference to Muslim identity politics, Modood (2010) offers a rebuttal of the view, now common among political groups in Western Europe, that Muslim assertiveness is incompatible with liberal democratic citizenship. He has a view of multicultural citizenship in which respect for difference is grounded in universalist values – a concept of political multiculturalism based on the ideas of difference and equality. Without this understanding, multiculturalism seeks the goal of positive difference, and the means to achieve this involves appreciation of the reality of multiplicity and groupness and the building of group pride among those marked by negative difference and subject to racism (this theme relates to our research findings, examined in Chapters 3 and 4). Modood also raises the concept of multiculturalism as linked to a vision of citizenship that is not confined to the state but dispersed across society, compatible with multiple forms of groupness. This is sustained through dialogue, with plural forms of representation that do not take one group as the model to which all others have to conform, and is characterized by new, reformed national identities. Meer *et al.* (2010) explore this further through different kinds of social identities, for example, the Muslim face-veil or *niqab* that is a 'contested signifier' (Meer *et al.*, 2010: 84) in contemporary social and political life. In this instance, personal dress is about how women may be seen as reproducers of ethnic collectives and, by extension, how they may be characterized as reproducers of boundaries of national groups. (We highlighted this issue in Chapter 4.) Meer *et al.* maintain that headscarf-wearing can be viewed as consistent with the right accorded within a multicultural society to wear 'ethnic dress', such as the Sikh turban or Jewish *yarmulke*. This is reflected in the protection from religious discrimination extended through anti-discrimination legislation in 2003 (specifically the Race Relations Act 1976 (Amendment) Regulations 2003).

Importantly, Meer *et al.* (2010) observe that until the late 1980s and early 1990s, Muslim identities were a minor feature of mainstream accounts of ethnic minorities and discourses of multiculturalism in Britain. After the Rushdie Affair (1988), which was a strong and at times violent reaction by some Muslims in the UK and elsewhere to Rushdie's novel *The Satanic Verses* because it was perceived as blasphemous (Qureshi and Khan, 1989), discourses highlighted the fact that minorities may subscribe not just to a national identity or a South Asian regionalism, but a potentially universal Muslim identity that provides a new form of self-identification and public claims-making. As such, difference on the basis of religious identity has formed part of recent debates about the nature of multiculturalism. Yuval-Davis (2009) proposed a discourse around the concept of 'multifaithism', suggesting that 'it has become the only legitimized difference within the nation' (Yuval-Davis, 2009: 134). Modood (2010) contends that this is a relatively new concept, used in an ad hoc manner and yet to be subjected to theoretical discussion and scrutiny. Nor has multifaithism been taken up as a shift from multicultural frameworks. For Modood, the new concept would act as an enhancement rather than a replacement of multiculturalism. However, the introduction of new concepts adds to the increasing discourse around religion rather than just ethnic/national origin as a significant aspect of people's identity.

Conceptions of interculturalism have also been raised and positively contrasted with multiculturalism. Meer and Modood (2012) argue that some advocates of political interculturalism wish to emphasize its positive qualities in terms of encouraging communication, recognizing dynamic identities, promoting unity, and critiquing illiberal cultural practices. Importantly, some of the criticism of multiculturalism is rooted in an objection to earlier formulations that displayed precisely those elements deemed unsatisfactory when compared with interculturalism. However, Meer and Modood (2012) argue that until interculturalism as a political discourse is able to offer a distinct perspective – one that can respond to a variety of issues emerging from complex identities – it cannot, intellectually at least, eclipse the ideology of multiculturalism. As such, these authors consider the concept of interculturalism as complementary to multiculturalism.

The appeal of multiculturalism as a public policy has suffered considerable political damage, with claims that it has failed to deliver a more equitable society. There are also claims that it has failed to take into consideration socio-economic inequalities (Hanson, 2006), and that it is to be blamed for international terrorism (Phillips, 2006). Meer and Modood (2011) argue that, while these political positions add to anxieties over multiculturalism, there have been benefits from the policy, and they point to the promotion of national unity and greater recognition of diversity. Further, they add that it is often unclear what precisely is being criticized and that even when critics say that what they are discussing is 'state multiculturalism', nothing is said about what this is, or how it differs from 'multiculturalism', before detractors go on to show why it is questionable.

Where do faith schools fit in a post-multicultural society?

We began our project in the context of community cohesion which is associated with the previous Labour government, and the agenda is now moving to policies on integration and cohesion in a broad sense. The future of faith-based education, and its coherence and alignment with national priorities in education, needs to be a key area of discussion.

Changes in government policy with regard to faith schools over the last 16 years have focused on inclusion and linkage. This was seen as an attempt by a Labour government to bring Muslim schools into the mainstream in 1998, and to award Muslim schools with the same status as Christian and Jewish schools. A further initiative was to encourage faith schools to demonstrate how they link with the wider community. As regards what these schools have been doing in terms of promoting cohesion and links with the wider community, our research found that there were a number of examples and they were taking place *before* the government directive to demonstrate engagement with the wider community in 2007 (DCSF, 2007a), as highlighted earlier. Examples of this practice included inter-school visits, interfaith religious festivals and charity donations, and volunteer work within and beyond their own faith group.

Policy on community relations in the UK and the role of schools in supporting the government agenda on promoting greater cohesion have now reached an impasse. The focus has been on faith schools, which have been criticized for adopting an isolationist stance – with Muslim schools, in particular, attracting criticism (Finney and Simpson, 2009). Further, as stated previously, there has been a move away from the concept of multiculturalism toward community cohesion (Cantle, 2006) as an ideology within the liberal state (MacMullen, 2007). The failure of multiculturalism to deliver equitable outcomes in society and an attempt to look beyond this concept are echoed elsewhere, for example, in Hollinger's (1995) *Post Ethnic America: Beyond Multiculturalism* and Kincheloe and Steinberg's (1997) work on critical multiculturalism. More recently, there have been political statements concerning France (Murray, 2006), Germany (Friedman, 2010), and the UK (Meer and Modood, 2009) to the effect that multiculturalism has failed. Given this alleged failure (Kudani, 2002; Kymlicka, 2012; Shome, 2012) there is disagreement as to whether it can, or should, be revived. As such, beyond community cohesion and failed multiculturalism is a policy vacuum. This raises implications for policy across education systems in Europe and beyond that seek to respond to the reality of how the dynamic of cultural identity and citizenship expresses itself in schools.

Moving forward, education needs to be viewed as both a preservative and a reproductive process. There is also a need for a fresh perspective, new language, and a new policy framework that reconceptualizes a nuanced understanding of multiculturalism and community cohesion.

The raison d'être of faith schools is to preserve religious faith. Their pupils are thus caught in the intersections between the different 'cultural scripts' of school and home (Devine, 2011: 165), and when these two environments overlap well, the conflict can be diminished. If faith schools are to respond to government initiatives in the future, the cultural script needs to be acknowledged as well as the experience of hostility from the wider community (Parker-Jenkins and Glenn, 2011). This involves an acknowledgement of anti-Semitism and Islamophobia and other racist behaviour. Children are particularly vulnerable to this, and parents in general select faith schools to avoid the experience of hostility, as we found in our case study. Racism is an issue that needs attention at both the government and the school level, and requires not only a statement of intent or mission but also a clear strategy and review of practice.

Miller (2011) notes that British Jews are facing new and complicated challenges as they grapple with the issues associated with relating to the

Conclusion

world around them. Importantly, she states that this challenge is not a phenomenon restricted to the Jewish schools of Britain, but the concept of schools and their relationships with the wider community is one that is particularly preoccupying the British government in the broad sense. A further challenge 'is one of balance ... [which provides for] integrating without assimilating' (Miller, 2011: 40).

The challenge for Jewish schools, she continues, is to develop young people who want to remain within a strong Jewish framework, but also to connect them to the wider world. She feels there is difficulty appreciating 'the possibilities of integration without assimilation' (ibid.). This is a particular problem 'for strictly orthodox schools that seek to develop graduates who are deeply knowledgeable about Jewish text, values and practice, and who principally lead their lives within a strictly orthodox community' (ibid.). Miller adds that:

> ... unfortunately, ignorance and mistrust of our neighbours are two of the biggest challenges to building cohesion and schools need help in learning how to play a role in building a mutual citizenship among different groups as well as ensuring respect for diversity.
>
> (ibid.: 42)

Putting values into practice is not simple, and whose agenda school stakeholders are following is not always clear. In the UK, there are competing agendas in relation to community cohesion and engagement. On the one hand, notes Miller (2011), many individuals and groups within wider British society view faith schools as obstacles to community cohesion or engagement. Alternatively, faith schools are perceived as 'a positive force for community cohesion and engagement' (ibid.).

Added to the backlash against multiculturalism, Muslim schools and communities have become more exposed to public scrutiny (Werbner, 2009) and accusations of posing a threat to social cohesion in Britain ('Lessons in Hate and Violence', 2011).

Berkeley and Sevita (2008) argue that faith schools are coming under greater scrutiny as they are being asked to play a more prominent role in the community and prepare pupils to be active citizens and effective participants in the labour market. Furthermore, the strategic direction of faith schools must strike a balance between cohesion, diversity, and equality. Berkeley and Sevita suggest a number of ways in which this could be done: (i) end selection on the basis of faith – faith schools should be open to all citizens and must value all young people, particularly those from disadvantaged backgrounds; (ii) Religious Education (RE) should be part of the national curriculum – the current provision of RE beyond the faith in faith schools is inadequate; and (iii) faith should continue to play an important role in our education system – such schools should offer choice to parents and diversity in schooling as a way of improving standards. Berkeley and Sevita also highlight that although debate about faith schools is often characterized by discussion of Muslim schools, there are very few Muslim schools in the state-maintained sector – currently 11 VA out of over 3,000 funded faith schools (DfE, 2012b). For Berkeley and Sevita (2008), the debate surrounding faith schools places too much emphasis on parental choice while children's views are virtually ignored. Berkeley and Sevita go on to stress that giving young people the opportunities to shape their own education is crucial in helping them develop the ability for critical thinking and self-determination.

What is notable in our analysis of group identity when discussing Jewish and Muslim communities is that we are problematizing the notion that group identities have singular meaning. Hopkins (2011: 533) highlights the fact that faith identities are typically depicted as fixed or uniform. However, a more discursive construction of identity underlines the view, as Bald *et al.* (2010) note, that religious identities are 'sites of ongoing contestation and struggle'. In a report for the Policy Exchange by these authors, it was claimed that the British education system is seen as ill equipped to deal with the challenges posed by the increasing vulnerability of Britain's faith schools in the face of extremist influences. Furthermore, Britain is perceived as lagging behind other liberal European democracies in addressing these problems, and the report's authors advise that the DfE and Ofsted could create a dedicated Due Diligence Unit within the Department. As such, those seeking to set up new schools should be assessed at each stage; a commitment to British values of democracy, tolerance, and patriotism should be part of the ethos of every school, and British history should be a compulsory part of the school curriculum. The Policy Exchange expresses a concern that faith schools do not actively promote British values or tolerance of other cultures, which is seen, on occasion, to contribute to a failure to prepare pupils for life in modern Britain. Islam-based institutions are regarded as particularly problematic and antithetical to the basic values of tolerance and secular democracy. However, as we have suggested throughout this book, the disproportionate attention that faith schools receive regarding cohesion is frequently grounded in a lack of knowledge of what takes place in these schools. Francis and Robbins's study is a notable exception, finding that:

> Overall, faith schools are concerned with enabling pupils to reflect on ultimate questions, to think critically about religion, and to understand the influence of religion in society, rather than shaping the religious and spiritual commitment of their pupils.
>
> (2011: 231)

Simplistic policies on multiculturalism do not do justice to the complexity and significance of identity based on ethnic, religious, linguistic, class, or sectarian background. In the current economic climate it is easy to move away from recognizing difference and developing social harmony, as evidenced by the abandoning – after only five years – of schools' obligation to evidence their promotion of the community cohesion agenda (DfE, 2012b). As our proposed model in Chapter 5 demonstrates, only short-term or tokenistic strategies are likely to have been achieved in the last five years or so, rather than a committed, long-term, substantive, and sustainable strategy toward some measure of genuine community engagement.

Looking to the future

Schools that have developed good practice in reaching out to the wider community may sustain policy in this area. For others, the competing commands of accountability, assessment, and league tables will provide ample validation for abandoning the community cohesion policy (DCSF, 2007a). Yet the issue still remains as to how all schools, not just faith schools, should engage with the wider community.

Finney and Simpson (2009) argue that a diverse society should not be seen as a threat, and note that Muslims are singled out as having behaviours potentially undesirable for British society. Further, the responsibility for ensuring they 'fit in' lies with the minorities themselves (Finney and Simpson, 2009: 95). This is a clear movement away from the talk of equality and celebration of cultural diversity of previous decades (Lynch, 1987; Craft and Bardell, 1984) and toward a perspective in which diversity is seen as undesirable (Letki, 2008). Further, 'by requiring behavioral change as the measure of integration, the "new" approach harks back to assimilationist ideologies and societies' (Finney and Simpson, 2009: 95). If an assimilationist agenda dictates that responsibility for integration rests exclusively on the shoulders of minorities, this is likely to be rejected. In short:

> The concern is about newcomers, both new immigrants and children of former immigrants (ethnic minorities), in particular those who may therefore upset the applecart of the accepted ways of life.
>
> (ibid.: 143)

This raises implications for education policy in the UK, which seeks to respond to the reality of how the dynamics of cultural identity and citizenship express themselves in schools. It is time for a new language and a new approach in responding to the reality of a multicultural society and global mobility. There is no easy solution, but according to Finney and Simpson people do not choose *not* to integrate:

> A spotlight on fair treatment, choice in housing, positive social behaviour, job availability and neighbourliness in areas that are changing their composition are more relevant to the goal of an integrated society. Britain's changing ethnic composition, both nationally and locally, is evident and important, but it does not of itself constitute a problem.
>
> (2009: 137)

Diversity on the basis of income and cultural background exists regardless of ethnic pluralism, but there are 'fears that skin colour and diversity are threats to social cohesion' with an emphasis on 'racial stereotyping' (ibid.: 156). Some literature asserts that some minority groups fear that integration means losing personal and cultural identity, and that is not acceptable to Jewish (Miller, 2011) or Muslim communities (Abbas, 2011).

Concluding remarks

We need a fresh approach to multiculturalism which is both sensitive and sensible. There have been calls for a more 'muscular or aggressive form of multiculturalism' (Latour, 2012, section 20) and, in the words of Prime Minister David Cameron, 'a lot less of the passive tolerance of recent years and a much more active, muscular liberalism', promoting the notion that 'to belong here is to believe and adhere to our shared British values of what it is to be British' (ibid.: section 22). There is fear of Sharia law (Bhala, 2011), which is seen as being opposed to what is valued in Britain, and certain strands of Islam which preach intolerance, for example of homosexuality, are criticized for being unacceptable in a British context. As part of this, there is a perceived fear of standing up to Muslim intolerance and aspects of Sharia law. However, to define all Muslims as intolerant is clearly wrong.

Conclusion

The tension lies in hearing alternative views and safeguarding cherished aspects of British culture. When we talk about multiculturalism, the debate is invariably in terms of Muslims (Firsing, 2012). Writers such as Kaplan (2013) and Kressel (2007) suggest that the debate needs to be broadened by discussing the fear of religious extremism in any form as a menace to society, for example, ultra-Zionists or anti-abortionists within the Jewish or Catholic communities. Similarly, the wider community needs to see cultural diversity as a resource on which to draw. Schools that are able to go beyond tokenistic, superficial approaches to encouraging meaningful engagement between communities can produce strong educational outcomes and strong communities.

As well as robust and enlightened policy at government level, we propose a framework for schools to continue reaching out to communities, within a community engagement approach. There is a policy vacuum in the post-community cohesion era, as stated earlier, and the Big Society message is confused. Logically, schools need to consider what Miller (2011) calls the balance between 'diversity and conformity', and that, moving forward, they can maintain a commitment to foster harmonious relations, breaking down stereotypes of other religious groups and those of no faith.

We have shown how Jewish and Muslim faith schools have strong conceptions of community, which, along a continuum, are used to engage and strengthen levels of education. As noted in Chapter 5 (Figure 1), community engagement can operate at a number of levels: from meaningful engagement where there is interaction through ongoing and sustained projects, to superficial engagement or no reaching-out whatsoever. Faith schools work hard through formal and informal curricula to preserve their cultural heritage, tradition, values, and practices, and to sustain them within educational environments. Schools are not neutral spaces and government agendas to change societal norms may be in conflict with those of the school community.

Religious and ethnic communities have different capacities, in terms of both financial and social capital, to mobilize and influence. The trend has now shifted from multiculturalism to the promotion of shared values and national security as a means to enhance community cohesion. There is also a shift from welcoming minority faith schools to viewing them with suspicion, as noted in the discussions throughout this book. Bridging gulfs between people through sophisticated and embedded forms of engagement, underpinned by government policy, is part of the way forward. There is responsibility on all sides. Faith schools aim to provide children with a roadmap for their lives, but they should not have license to deny the children in their care access to knowledge and appropriate links in order to reach out and learn about, from, and with their peers. This will be vital if they are to be ready for living, working, and leading in the twenty-first century.

Bibliography

Abbas, T. (2011) *Islam and Education*. London: Routledge.

Abdul-Rahman, S.M. (2007) *Islam: Questions and answers – jurisprudence and Islamic rulings*. London: MSA.

Abrams, F. (2011) 'Islamic schools flourish to meet demand'. *The Guardian*, 28 November. Online. www.theguardian.com/education/2011/nov/28/muslim-schools-growth (accessed 28 November 2013).

ACT (Association for Citizenship Teaching) (2012) 'The secondary curriculum'. Online. www.teachingcitizenship.org.uk/about-citizenship/citizenship-curriculum/secondary-curriculum (accessed 1 May 2014).

Akhtar, S. (1993) *The Muslim Parents' Handbook: What every Muslim parent should know*. London: Ta Ha.

Al-Attas, M.N. (ed.) (1979) *Aims and Objectives of Islamic Education*. London: Hodder & Stoughton.

Alexander, H.A. and McLaughlin, T.H. (2003) 'Education in religion and spirituality'. In N. Blake, P. Smeyers, R. Smith and P. Standish (eds), *The Blackwell Guide to the Philosophy of Education*. Oxford: Blackwell, 356–73.

Alibhai-Brown, Y. (2000) *After Multiculturalism*. London: Foreign Policy Centre.

Allen, C. (2007) *The 'First' Decade of Islamophobia: 10 years of the Runnymede Trust report 'Islamophobia: A challenge for us all'*. Stourbridge: Chris Allen.

—— (2010) *Islamophobia*. 1st ed. Farnham: Ashgate.

Allen, C. and Nielsen, J. (2002) *Summary Report on Islamophobia in the EU After 11 September 2001*. Vienna: European Monitoring Centre on Racism and Xenophobia.

Allen, R. (2008) 'Choice-based Secondary School Admissions in England: Social stratification and the distribution of educational outcomes.' Unpublished PhD thesis, Institute of Education, University of London. Online. http://eprints.ioe.ac.uk/632/ (accessed 3 February 2014).

Allen, R. and Vignoles, A. (2010) *Can School Competition Improve Standards?: The case of faith schools in England*. London: Institute of Education, University of London. Online. http://repec.ioe.ac.uk/REPEc/pdf/qsswp0904.pdf (accessed 27 Feburary 2014).

Alliance Party (2010) 'Draft Programme for Cohesion, Sharing and Integration: Consultation Response from the Alliance Party of Northern Ireland'. Online. www.ofmdfmni.gov.uk/csiresponses2010_alliance_party_of_northern_ireland.pdf (accessed 29 June 2014).

Allport, G. (1954) *The Nature of Prejudice*. Reading, MA: Addison-Wesley.

AMS UK (n.d.) 'Association of Muslim Schools'. Online. www.ams-uk.org (accessed 6 April 2014).

Ananiadou, K. and Claro, M. (2009) '21st century skills and competences for new millennium learners in OECD countries'. *OECD Education Working Papers*, 41. Paris: OECD. Online. http://dx.doi.org/10.1787/218525261154 (accessed 22 May 2014).

Anwar, M. (2005) 'Muslims in Britain: Issues, policies and practices'. In T. Abbas (ed.), *Communities under Pressure*. London: Zed Books.

Apple, M. (2012) 'Social structure, ideology and curriculum'. In M. Lawn, and L. Barton (eds), *Rethinking Curriculum Studies*. Abingdon: Routledge.

Apple, M., Au, W., and Gandin, L.A. (2011) *The Routledge Book of Critical Education*. London: Routledge.

Archbishop's Council Church Schools Review Group (2001) *The Way Ahead: Church of England schools in the new millennium, chaired by Lord R. Dearing*. London: Church House Publishing.

Archer, L. and Francis, B. (2007) *Understanding Minority Ethnic Achievement: Race, class and gender*. London: Routledge.

Armitage, W.H.G. (1964) *Four Hundred Years of English Education*. Cambridge: Cambridge University Press.

Arthur, J. (1995) 'Government Education Policy and Voluntary-Aided Schools'. *Oxford Review of Education*, 11 (1), 447–55.

Arthur, J., Gardner, R., and Cairns, J. (2005) *Measuring Catholic School Performance: An international perspective*. London: RoutledgeFalmer.

Ashraf, S.A. (1993) 'The role of Muslim youth in a multi-religious society'. *Muslim Education Quarterly*, 11 (1), 3–13.

Bagguley, P. and Hussain, Y. (2008) *Riotous Citizens: Ethnic conflict in multicultural Britain*. Aldershot: Ashgate.

Bald, J., Harber, A., Robinson, N., and Schiff, E. (2010) *Faith Schools We Can Believe In: Ensuring that tolerant and democratic values are upheld in every part of Britain's education system*. London: Policy Exchange.

Banting, K. and Kymlicka, W. (2010) *Multiculturalism Policy Index*. Online. www.queensu.ca/mcp (accessed 2 June 2013).

Barber, M., Donnelly, K., and Rizvi, S. (2012) *Oceans of Innovation: The Atlantic, the Pacific, global leadership and the future of education*. London: Institute for Public Policy Research.

Barth, F. (1969) *Ethnic Groups and Boundaries: The social organisation of cultural difference*. London: George Allen and Unwin.

BBC News (2010) 'Muslim parents "banning children from music lessons"'. Online. http://news.bbc.co.uk/local/london/hi/people_and_places/religion_and_ethics/newsid_8780000/8780567.stm (accessed 22 May 2014).

—— (2009) 'Ofsted checks on school extremism', 9 March. Online. http://news.bbc.co.uk/1/hi/education/7933486.stm (accessed 9 March 2009).

Beckerman, Z. and McGlynn, C. (2007) *Addressing Ethnic Conflict Through Peace Education: International perspectives*. New York: Palgrave Macmillan.

Berg, B. (2001) *Qualitative Research Methods for the Social Sciences*, 4th ed. London: Allyn and Bacon.

Berger, M., Galonska, C., and Koopmans, R. (2004) 'Political integration by a detour?: Ethnic communities and social capital of migrants in Berlin'. *Journal of Ethnic and Migration Studies*, 30 (3), 491–507.

Berglund, J. (2011) 'Global questions in the classroom: The formation of Islamic religious education in Sweden'. *Discourse: Studies in the Cultural Politics of Education*, 32 (4), 497–512.

Berkeley, R. and Sevita, V. (2008) *Right to Divide?: Faith schools and community cohesion*. London: Runnymede Trust. Online. www.runnymedetrust.org/uploads/publications/pdfs/RightToDivide-2008.pdf (accessed 3 February 2009).

Bibliography

Bhala, R. (2011) 'Understanding Islamic law (Sharia)'. Online. https://law.drupal.ku.edu/sites/law.drupal.ku.edu/files/docs/resources/library/IslamicLawResearch.pdf (accessed 22 May 2014).

Black, J. (1998) *JFS: The History of the Jews' Free School, London since 1732*. London: Tymsder.

Bloemberg, L. and Nijhuis, D. (1993) 'Hindoescholen in Nederland [Hindu schools in the Netherlands]'. *Migrantenstudies*, 9, 35–52.

Bolton, P. and Gillie, C. (2009) 'Faith Schools: Admissions and Performance'. Online. www.parliament.uk/business/publications/research/briefing-papers/SN04405/faith-schools-admissions-and-performance (accessed 29 June 2014).

Booth, T. and Ainscow, M. (2002) *Index for Inclusion: Developing learning and participation in schools*. Bristol: Centre for Studies on Inclusive Education.

Bourdieu, P. (1985) 'The social space and the genesis of groups'. *Theory and Society*, 14, 723–44.

Brah, A. (1996) *Cartographies of Diasporas: Contesting identities*. London: Routledge.

Brighouse, H. (2006) *On Education*. London: Routledge.

British Humanist Association (2002) *A Better Way Forward: BHA policy on religion and schools*. London: British Humanist Association. Online. www.humanism.org.uk/wp-content/uploads/Betterwayforward2006.pdf (accessed 25 November 2012).

Brown, A. (2003) 'Church of England schools: Politics, power, identity'. *British Journal of Religious Education*, 25 (2), 103–16.

Bruce, S., Glendinning, T., Paterson, I., and Rosie, M. (2005) 'Religious discrimination in Scotland: Fact or myth?'. *Ethnic and Racial Studies*, 28 (1), 151–68.

Bryant, A. and Charmaz, K. (2010) *The SAGE Handbook of Grounded Theory*. Thousand Oaks, CA: Sage.

Bryk, A., Lee, V., and Holland, P. (1993) *Catholic Schools and the Common Good*. Cambridge, MA: Harvard University Press.

Burgess, S., Greaves, E., Vignoles, A., and Wilson, D. (2009) 'Parental choice of primary schools in England: What "type" of school do parents want?', Working Paper 09/224. Bristol: University of Bristol Centre for Market and Public Organisation. Online. www.bristol.ac.uk/cmpo/publications/papers/2009/wp224.pdf (accessed 21 March 2014).

Burnett, J. (2004) 'Community, cohesion and the state'. *Race and Class*, 45 (1), 1–17.

Burtonwood, N. (2003) 'Social cohesion, autonomy and the liberal defence of faith schools'. *Journal of Philosophy of Education*, 37 (3), 415–25.

Cairns, E. and Darby, J. (1998) 'Conflict in Northern Ireland: Causes, consequences, and controls'. *American Psychologist*, 53 (7), 754–60.

Cantle, T. (2006) 'Parallel lives'. *Index on Censorship*, 35 (2), 85–90.

Canuto, M.-A. and Yaeger, J. (2000) *The Archaeology of Communities: A new world perspective*. London: Routledge.

Carr, J., and Haynes, A. (2013) 'A clash of racialisations: The policing of "race" and of anti-Muslim racism in Ireland'. *Critical Sociology*. Published online only. http://crs.sagepub.com/content/early/2013/07/05/0896920513492805. abstract?patientinform-links=yes&legid=spcrs;0896920513492805v1 (requires subscription). Accessed 27 February 2014.

Carroll, P. (2003) 'Race and citizenship after 2000: Educational policy and practice'. Unpublished PhD thesis, University of Southampton.

CES (Catholic Education Service) (1997) *The Catholic Schools and Other Faiths Report*. London: CES.

—— (1998) *Education for Love*. London: CES.

—— (1999) *Evaluating the Distinctive Nature of the Catholic School*, 4th ed. London: CES.

—— (2000) *Performance Management*. London: CES.

—— (2003) *Ethnicity, Identity and Achievement in Catholic Education*. London: CES.

—— (2012) *Digest of 2011 Census Data for Schools and Colleges*. London: CES.

CBS (2011) *Jaarboek Onderwijs in Cijfers 2011*. Den Haag: Centraal Bureau voor de Statistiek.

Cheong, P.H., Edwards, R., Goulbourne, H., and Solomos, J. (2005) 'Immigration, social cohesion and social capital: A critical review'. Paper presented at the 'Whiter Social Capital? Past, present and future' conference, London, 6–7 April.

Cherti, M. and Bradley, L. (2011) *Inside Madrassas: Understanding and engaging with British-Muslim faith supplementary schools*. London: Institute for Public Policy Research.

Choudhury, T., Malik, M., Halstead, J.M., Bunglawala, Z., and Spalek, B. (2005) *Muslims in the UK: Policies for engaged citizens*. Budapest: Open Society Institute.

Church, C., Visser, A., and Johnson, L.S. (2004) 'A path to peace or persistence?: The "single identity" approach to conflict resolution in Northern Ireland'. *Conflict Resolution Quarterly*, 21 (3), 273–93.

Church Schools Review Group (2001) *The Way Ahead: Church of England schools in the new millennium*. London: Church House Publishing. Online. www.churchofengland.org/media/1118777/way%20ahead%20-%20whole.pdf (accessed 24 July 2014).

Coffin, E.A. and Bolozky, S. (2005) *A Reference Grammar of Modern Hebrew*. Cambridge, Cambridge University Press.

Cohen L., Manion, L., and Morrison, K. (2000) *Research Methods in Education*. London: Open Books.

—— (2008) *Research Methods in Education*, 6th ed. London: Routledge.

COIC (Commission on Integration and Cohesion) (2007) *Interim Statement from the Commission on Integration and Cohesion*. Coventry: Department for Communities and Local Government.

Coleman, J.S. (1994) *Foundations of Social Theory*. Cambridge, MA: Belknap Press.

Commission on British Muslims and Islamophobia (1997) *Islamophobia: A challenge for us all*. London: Runnymede Trust.

—— (2001) *Addressing the Challenge of Islamophobia: Progress Report, 1999–2001*. London: Commission on British Muslims and Islamophobia.

Bibliography

Commission on Integration and Cohesion (2007) *Our Interim Statement*. London: Department for Communities and Local Government.

—— (2007) *Our Shared Future*. Wetherby: Commission on Integration and Cohesion.

Communities and Local Government (2010) *All-Party Inquiry into Antisemitism: Government response – three years on progress report*. London: The Stationery Office.

CST (Community Security Trust) (2007) *Antisemitic Incidents Report 2007*. London: CST. Online. www.thecst.org.uk/docs/Incidents_Report_07.pdf (accessed 1 April 2008).

—— (2010) *Antisemitic Incidents Report 2010*. London: CST. Online. www.thecst.org.uk/docs/Incidents%20Report%202010.pdf (accessed 1 May 2014).

—— (2012) *Antisemitic Incidents Report 2012*. London: CST. Online. www.thecst.org.uk/docs/Incidents%20Report%202012.pdf (accessed 6 May 2014).

—— (2013) *Antisemitic Incidents Report 2013*. London: CST. Online. www.thecst.org.uk/docs/Incidents%20Report%202013.pdf (accessed 6 May 2014).

Conroy, J.C. (2001) 'A very Scottish affair: Catholic education and the state'. *Oxford Review of Education*, 27 (4), 543–58.

Conroy, J.C. and McCreath, D. (1999) 'The challenge to Catholic teacher education in Scotland'. *Catholic Education: A journal of inquiry and practice*, 2 (3), 312–27.

Conway, D. (2009) *Disunited Kingdom: How the government's community cohesion agenda undermines British identity and nationhood*. London: Civitas. Online. www.civitas.org.uk/pdf/DisunitedKingdom.pdf (accessed 2 June 2013).

Copley, T. (2005) *Indoctrination, Education and God: The struggle for the mind*. London: Society for Promoting Christian Knowledge.

Council of Europe (1947) 'The European Convention on Human Rights'. Online. www.hri.org/docs/ECHR50.html (accessed 6 May 2014).

Craft, M. and Bardell, G. (eds) (1984) *Curriculum Opportunities in a Multicultural Society*. London: Harper Educational.

Curtis, S.J. and Boultwood, M.E. (1966) *An Introductory History of English Education Since 1800*, 4th ed. London: University Tutorial Press.

Cush, D. (2003) 'Should the State fund schools with a religious character?' *Religious Education (PCfRE)*, 25 (2), 10–15.

Cush, D. and Francis, D. (2002) '"Positive pluralism" to awareness, mystery and value: A case study in religious education curriculum development'. *British Journal of Religious Education*, 24 (1), 52–67.

Dadzi, S. (2001) *Toolkit for Tackling Racism in Schools*. Stoke-on-Trent: Trentham Books.

Dagovitz, A. (2004) 'When choice does not matter: Political liberalism, religion and the faith school debate'. *Journal of Philosophy of Education*, 38 (2), 165–80.

Davis, S. (1999) 'From moral duty to cultural rights: A case study of political framing in education'. *Sociology of Education*, 27 (1), 1–21.

Dawkins, R. (2001) 'No faith in the absurd'. *Times Educational Supplement*, 23 February: 17.

DCLG (Department for Communities and Local Government) (2010) *The Training and Development of Muslim Faith Leaders: Current practice and future possibilities*. London: DCLG.

DCSF (Department for Children, Schools and Families) (2007a) *Guidance on the Duty to Promote Community Cohesion*. London: DCSF. Online. http://webarchive.nationalarchives.gov.uk/20130401151715/http://www.education.gov.uk/publications/eOrderingDownload/DCSF-00598-2007.pdf (accessed 29 April 2014).

—— (2007b) *The Children's Plan: Building brighter futures*. London: DCSF. Online. http://webarchive.nationalarchives.gov.uk/20130401151715/https://www.education.gov.uk/publications/standard/_arc_SOP/Page11/CM%207280 (accessed 29 April 2014).

Declaration of the Rights of Man and of the Citizen (1789) Online. http://chnm.gmu.edu/revolution/d/295/ (accessed 6 May 2014).

Deer, C. (2005) 'Faith Schools in France: From conflict to consensus?'. In R. Gardner, J. Cairns, and D. Lawton (eds), *Faith Schools: Consensus or conflict?* London: RoutledgeFalmer.

Denham, J. (2001) *Building Cohesive Communities: A report of the ministerial group on public order and community cohesion*. London: Home Office.

Denzin, N.K. and Lincoln, Y.S. (2002) *The SAGE Handbook of Qualitative Research*. Thousand Oaks, CA: Sage.

Department for Innovation, Universities and Skills (2008) *Promoting Good Campus Relations: Fostering shared values and preventing extremism in universities and higher education colleges*. London: DIUS.

Department of Education Northern Ireland (2012) 'Pupil attendance'. Online. www.deni.gov.uk/index/32-statisticsandresearch_pg/32-statistics_and_research_statistics_on_education_pg/32_statistics_and_research_-_statistics_on_education-pupil_attendance.htm (accessed 24 February 2014).

Desforges, C. (2003) *The Impact of Parental Involvement, Parental Support and Family Education on Pupil Achievements and Adjustment: A literature review*. London: DfES.

Devine, D. (2011) *Immigration and Schooling in the Republic of Ireland: Making a difference?*. Manchester: Manchester University Press.

Dewey, J. (1916) *Democracy and Education*. New York: Free Press.

DfE (Department for Education) (2010a) *Maintained Faith Schools*. London: Department for Education.

—— (2010b) *The Importance of Teaching: The schools white paper*. London: Department for Education.

—— (2011) *Improving the Spiritual, Moral, Social and Cultural (SMCC) Development of Pupils: Non-statutory guidance for independent schools*. Online. http://dera.ioe.ac.uk/id/eprint/12488 (accessed 6 May 2014).

—— (2012a) 'Changes to inspection in January 2012'. Online. www.usethekey.org.uk/school-evaluation-and-improvement-/inspection/whole-school-inspection-criteria/proposed-changes-to-inspection-under-the-coalition-government (accessed 3 December 2012).

—— (2012b) 'Voluntary and faith schools'. Online. www.education.gov.uk/schools/leadrship/types of schools/maintained/b0001988369/voluntaryschools (accessed 12 June 2013).

—— (2014) *Health and safety: Advice on legal duties and powers, for local authorities, school leaders, school staff and governing bodies*. Online. http://dera.ioe.ac.uk/id/eprint/19588 (accessed 6 April 2014).

—— (n.d.) 'EduBase'. Online. www.education.gov.uk/edubase.home.xhtml (accessed 6 May 2014).
DfEE (Department for Education and Employment) (2001) *Schools: Building on success*. Norwich: HMSO. Online. www.gov.uk/government/uploads/system/uploads/attachment_data/file/250873/5050.pdf (accessed 29 April 2014).
DfES (Department for Education and Skills) (2006a) *Religious Education in Faith Schools*. London: DfES.
—— (2006b) *Making Places in Faith Schools Available to Other Faiths*. London: DfES.
Dijkstra, A.B., Dronkers, J., and Karsten, S. (2004) 'Private schools as public provision for education: School choice and market forces in the Netherlands'. In P.J. Wolf and S. Macedo (eds), *Educating Citizens: International perspectives on civic values and school choice*. Washington D.C.: Brookings Institution Press.
Dodd, V. (2010) 'Police demand new powers to stop and search terror suspects', *The Guardian*, 29 December. Online. www.theguardian.com/uk/2010/dec/29/police-stop-and-search-powers (accessed 12 August 2014).
Dronkers, J., Felouzis, G., and Zanten, A.V. (2010) 'Education markets and school choice'. *Educational Research and Evaluation: An International Journal on Theory and Practice*, 16 (2), 99–105.
Dunn, K.M., Klocker, N., and Salabay, T. (2007) 'Contemporary racism and Islamophobia in Australia: Racializing religion'. *Ethnicities*, 7 (4), 564–89.
Dwyer, C. (2008) 'The geographies of veiling: Muslim women in Britain'. *Geography*, 93 (3), 140–47.
Dwyer, C. and Uberoi, V. (2009) 'British Muslims and community cohesion debates'. In R. Phillips (ed.), *Muslim Spaces of Hope: Geographies of possibility in Britain and the West*. London: Zed Books.
Dyson, A. and Gallannaugh, F. (2008) 'Disproportionality in special needs education in England'. *Journal of Special Education*, 21 (1), 36–46.
Eaton, M., Longmore, J., and Naylor, A. (2000) *Commitment to Diversity: Catholics and education in a changing world*. London: Cassell.
The Economist (2013) 'Muslim education in Britain. Learning to live together, or separately.' 28 March. Online. www.economist.com/blogs/erasmus/2013/03/muslim-education-britain (accessed 28 March 2013).
Education Act (1944) Online. www.legislation.gov.uk/ukpga/Geo6/7-8/31/contents (accessed 6 May 2014).
—— (1996) Online. www.legislation.gov.uk/ukpga/1996/56/contents (accessed 6 May 2014).
—— (2002) Online. www.legislation.gov.uk/ukpga/2002/32/contents (accessed 6 May 2014).
Education and Inspections Act (2006) (Commencement No.6) Order 2007. London: HMSO. Online. www.opsi.gov.uk/si/si2007/uksi_20073074_en_1 (accessed 18 February 2009).
Education and Training Inspectorate (2009) 'An Evaluation of the Quality Assurance of Community Relations Funding in a Range of Formal and Non-formal Education Settings'. Online. www.etini.gov.uk/index/surveys-evaluations/surveys-evaluations-youth/surveys-evaluations-youth-2009/an-evaluation-of-the-quality-assurance-of-community-relations-funding-in-a-range-of-formal-and-non-formal-education-settings-youth.htm (accessed 2 July 2014).

Education Reform Act (1988) London: HMSO. Online. www.legislation.gov.uk/ukpga/1988/40 (accessed 29 April 2014).

Edwards, T., Gewirtz, S., and Whitty, G. (1993) *Specialisation and Choice in Urban Education: The City Technology College experiment*. London: Routledge.

Elchardus, M. and Kavadias, D. (2000) *The Socializing Effects of Educational Networks: The relevance of the distinction between public and private schools with relation to noncognitive outcomes of last year pupils in Flanders (Belgium)*. Brussels: Department of Sociology, Vrije Universiteit Brussel.

Elementary Education Act (1870) Online. www.educationengland.org.uk/documents/acts/1870-elementary-education-act.html (accessed 6 May 2014).

European Monitoring Centre on Racism and Xenophobia (2009: Now the European Forum on Antisemitism) 'Working definition of anti-Semitism'. Online. Now at www.european-forum-on-antisemitism.org/working-definition-of-antisemitism/english/ (accessed 1 May 2014).

Everett, H. (2012) 'Faith Schools and Tolerance: A comparative study of the influence of faith schools on students' attitudes of tolerance'. Unpublished PhD thesis, Institute of Education, University of London.

Exley, S. (2009) 'Exploring pupil segregation between specialist and non-specialist schools'. *Oxford Review of Education*, 35 (4), 451–70.

Faas, D. (2013) 'Ethnic diversity and schooling in national education systems'. *Education*, 4 (1), 5–10.

Feinberg, W. (1998) *Common Schools, Uncommon Identities: National unity and cultural difference*. New Haven, CT: Yale University Press.

Field, C. (2007) 'Islamophobia in contemporary Britain: The evidence of the opinion polls, 1988–2006'. *Islam and Christian–Muslim Relations*, 18 (4), 447–77.

Fielding, N. (2005) *The Police and Social Conflict*, 2nd ed. London: GlassHouse.

Find a Jewish School (n.d.) Online. www.findajewishschool.co.uk (accessed 6 May 2014).

Fineberg, M., Samuels, S., and Weitzman, M. (eds) (2007) *Antisemitism: The generic opinion*. Edgware: Valentine Mitchell.

Finney, N. and Simpson, L. (2009) *Sleepwalking to Segregation?: Challenging myths about race and migration*, 1st ed. Bristol: Policy Press.

Firsing, S. (2012) 'South Africa, the United States, and the fight against Islamic extremism'. *Democracy and Security*, 8 (1), 1–27.

Flint, J. (2007) 'Faith schools, multiculturalism and community cohesion: Muslims and Roman Catholic state schools in England and Scotland'. *Policy and Politics*, 35 (2), 251–68.

Florida, R., Knudsen, B., and Stolarick, K. (2005) 'The university and the creative economy'. In A. Araya and M.A. Peters (eds), *Education in the Creative Economy*. New York: Peter Lang, 45–77.

Forrest, R. and Kearns, A. (2001) 'Social cohesion, social capital and the neighbourhood'. *Urban Studies*, 38 (12), 2125–43.

Francis, L.J. and Lankshear, D.W. (2001) 'The relationship between church schools and local church life: Distinguishing between aided and controlled status'. *Educational Studies*, 24 (4), 425–38.

Bibliography

Francis, L.J. and Robbins, M. (2011) 'Teaching secondary RE at faith schools in England and Wales: Listening to the teachers'. *Journal of Beliefs and Values* 32, 219–33.

French Constitution of 4 October 1958. Online. www.conseil-constitutionnel.fr/conseil-constitutionnel/english/constitution/constitution-of-4-october-1958.25742.html (accessed 24 June 2014).

Friedman, G. (2010) 'Germany and the Failure of Multiculturalism'. *Geopolitical Weekly*, 19 October. Online. www.stratfor.com/weekly/20101018_germany_and_failure_multiculturalism (accessed 29 June 2014).

Furbey, R., Dinham, A., Farnell, R., Finneron, D., and Wilkinson, G., with Howarth, C., Hussain, D., and Palmer, S. (2006) *Faith as Social Capital: Connecting or dividing?* York: Joseph Rowntree Foundation.

Gaine, C. (1995) *Still No Trouble Here*. Stoke-on-Trent: Trentham Books.

—— (2005) *We're All White, Thanks: The persisting myth about 'white' schools*. Stoke-on-Trent: Trentham Books.

Gallagher, A.M. (1995) *Facets of the Conflict in Northern Ireland*. New York: St Martins Press.

Gallagher, E. and Cairns, E. (2011) 'National identity and in-group/out-group attitudes: Catholic and Protestant children in Northern Ireland'. *European Journal of Developmental Psychology*, 8 (1), 58–73.

Gallagher, T. (2004) *Education in Divided Societies*. New York: Palgrave Macmillan.

Gardner, R., Lawton, D., and Cairns, J. (eds) (2005) *Faith Schools: Consensus or conflict?*. London: RoutledgeFalmer.

Gardner Chadwick, K. (2004). *Improving Schools through Community Engagement: A practical guide for educators*. Thousand Oaks, CA: Corwin Press.

Gay, J.D. and Greenough, J. (2000) *The Geographical Distribution of Church Schools in England*. Oxford: Culham College Institute.

Gibbons, S., Machin, S., and Silva, O. (2008) 'Choice, competition and pupil attainment'. *Journal of European Economic Association*, 6 (4), 912–47.

Giddens, A. (1995) *Politics, Sociology and Social Theory: Encounters with classical and contemporary social thought*. Cambridge: Polity Press.

—— (2001) *Sociology*, 4th ed. Cambridge: Polity Press.

Gilby, N., Ormston, R., Parfrement, J., and Payne, C. (2011) *Amplifying the Voice of Muslim Students: Findings from literature review*. London: Department for Business, Innovation, and Skills.

Gillborn, D. (1995) *Racism and Antiracism in Real Schools*. Buckingham: Open University Press.

Gilliat-Ray, S. (2010) *Muslims in Britain: An introduction*. Cambridge: Cambridge University Press.

—— (2011) *Fieldwork in Religion: A guide for qualitative researchers*. London: Continuum.

Gilroy, P. (1993) *The Black Atlantic: Modernity and double consciousness*. London: Verso.

—— (1987) *There Ain't No Black in the Union Jack*. London: Hutchinson.

Giroux, H. and Purpel, D. (eds) (1983) *Hidden Curriculum and Moral Education: Deception or discovery?* Berkeley, CA: McCutchan.

Githens-Mazer, J. and Lambert, R. (2010) *Islamophobia and Anti-Muslim Hate-Crime: A London case study*. Exeter: University of Exeter.

Glaser, B.G. and Strauss, A.L. (1975) *The Discovery of Grounded Theory: Strategies for qualitative research*. New York: Aldine.

Gorard, S., Taylor, C., and Fitz, J. (2003) *Schools, Markets and Choice Policies*. London: RoutledgeFalmer.

Gov.uk (2014) 'Types of school'. Online. www.gov.uk/types-of-school/faith-schools (accessed 29 June 2014).

Grace, G. (2001) 'The State and Catholic schooling in England and Wales: Politics, ideology and mission integrity'. *Oxford Review of Education*, 27 (4), 489–500.

—— (2003) 'Educational studies and faith-based schooling: Moving from prejudice to evidence-based argument'. *British Journal of Educational Studies*, 51 (2), 149–67.

Graham, D. and Vulkan, D. (2010) *Synagogue Membership in the United Kingdom in 2010*. London: Board of Deputies and Institute for Jewish Policy Research.

Graham, D., Staesky, L., and Boyd, J. (2014) *Jews in the United Kingdom in 2013: Preliminary findings from the National Jewish Community Survey*. London: Institute for Jewish Policy Research.

Greeley, A. (1998) 'Catholic schools at the crossroads: An American perspective'. In M.M. Feheney (ed.), *From Ideal to Action: The inner nature of a Catholic school today*. Dublin: Veritas.

The Guardian (2001) 'Facts about faith schools', 14 November. Online. www.guardian.co.uk/education/2001/nov/14/schools.uk2 (accessed 26 November 2012).

Gunaratnam, Y. (2003) *Researching Race and Ethnicity: Methods, knowledge and power*. London: Sage.

Gunn, J. (2004) 'Religious freedom and *laïcité*: A comparison of the United States and France'. *BYU Law Review*, 2, 420–502.

Hadden, J.K. (1989) 'Desacralizing secularization theory'. In J.K. Hadden and A. Shupe (eds.), *Secularization and Fundamentalism Reconsidered*. New York: Paragon House.

Hajisoteriou, C. and Angelides, P. (2013) 'The politics of intercultural education in Cyprus: Policy-making and challenges'. *Education*, 4 (1), 103–23.

Hall, S. (1992) 'New Ethnicities'. In J. Donald and A. Rattanzi (eds), *Race, Culture and Difference*. London: Sage.

Halsall, J. (2012) 'Theorising the relationship between racial segregation and rioting'. *International Journal of Business and General Management*, 1 (2), 75–89.

Halstead, J.M. (2004) 'An Islamic concept of education'. *Comparative Education*, 40 (4), 517–29.

—— (2007) 'Islamic values: A distinct framework for moral education?'. *Journal of Moral Education*, 36 (3), 283–96.

Halstead, J.M. and McLaughlin, T. (2005) 'Are faith schools divisive?'. In R. Gardner, J. Cairns, and D. Lawton (eds), *Faith Schools: Consensus or conflict?*. London: Routledge.

Hammersley, M. and Atkinson, P. (2007) *Ethnography: Principles in practice*, 3rd ed. London: Routledge.

Bibliography

Haneef, S. (1979) *What Every Muslim Should Know about Islam and Muslims*. Lahore: Kazore.

Hanson, E.O. (2006) *Religion and Politics in the International System Today*. Cambridge: Cambridge University Press.

Harrison, M. (2004) *Integration and Social Sustainability: Developing a substitute for the top-down delusions of the community cohesion strategy, and creating appropriate research*. Leeds: University of Leeds.

Hattie, J. (2011) *Visible Learning for Teachers: Maximizing impact on learning*. London: Routledge.

Hattie, J. and Yates, G. (2011) 'Understanding learning: Lessons for learning, teaching and research'. Online. http://research.acer.edu.au/cgi/viewcontent.cgi?article=1207&context=research_conference (accessed 12 May 2014).

Haw, K. (2009) 'From hijab to jilbab and the "myth" of British identity: Being Muslim in contemporary Britain a half-generation on'. *Race, Ethnicity and Education*, 12 (3), 363–78.

Haydon, G. (ed.) (2009) *Faith in Education: A tribute to Terence McLaughlin*. London: Institute of Education.

Hayes, B.C. and McAlister, I. (2009a) 'Religion, identity and community relations among adults and young adults in Northern Ireland'. *Journal of Youth Studies*, 12 (4), 385–403.

—— (2009b) 'Education as a mechanism for conflict resolution in Northern Ireland'. *Oxford Review of Education*, 35 (4), 437–50.

Herald Scotland (2012) 'Muslim parents bid to set up private Islamic school'. 30 June. Online. www.heraldscotland.com/news/education/muslim-parents-bid-to-set-up-private-islamic-school.18015165 (accessed 6 May 2014).

Herbert, I. (2001) '"Apartheid" fears over first Muslim secondary school in state sector'. *The Independent*, 2 April: 11.

Hewer, C. (2001) 'Schools for Muslims'. *Oxford Review of Education*, 27 (4), 515–28.

Hick, J. (1995) *The Rainbow of Faiths: Critical dialogues on religious pluralism*. London: SCM Press.

Hickman, M. (1995) *Religion, Class and Identity: The State, the Catholic Church and the education of the Irish in Britain*. Aldershot: Avebury.

Hill, M. (2009) 'What the JFS ruling meant: A distinguished church lawyer asks what last week's Supreme Court defeat for the Chief Rabbi means for faith schools'. *The Guardian*, 21 December. Online. www.theguardian.com/commentisfree/belief/2009/dec/21/judaism-jfs-faith-schools-discrimination (accessed 22 May 2014).

HM Government (2011) 'Prevent Strategy'. London: HMSO. Online. https://www.gov.uk/government/uploads/system/uploads/attachment_data/file/97976/prevent-strategy-review.pdf (accessed 12 May 2014).

Hollinger, D. (1995). *Postethnic America: Beyond multiculturalism*. New York: Basic Books.

Home Office (2001a) *Building Cohesive Communities: A report of the ministerial group on public order and community cohesion*. London: The Stationery Office.

—— (2001b) *Schools Achieving Success*. White Paper. London: The Stationery Office.

—— (2003) *Community Cohesion Pathfinder Programme: The first six months*. London: Home Office.

—— (2004) *Community Cohesion Standards in Schools*. London: Home Office.

—— (2005) *Improving Opportunity, Strengthening Society: The government's strategy to increase race equality and community cohesion*. London: The Stationery Office.

—— (2006) *All-Party Parliamentary Inquiry into Anti-Semitism*. London: The Stationery Office.

—— (2011) *Prevent Strategy*. Online. www.gov.uk/government/uploads/system/uploads/attachment_data/file/97976/prevent-strategy-review.pdf (accessed 2 June 2013).

Hopkins, N. (2011) 'Religion and social capital: Identity matters'. *Journal of Community & Applied Social Psychology*, 21, 528–40.

Hornsby-Smith, M. (2000) 'The changing social and religious content of Catholic schooling in England and Wales'. In M. Eaton, J. Longnore, and A. Naylor (eds), *Commitment to Diversity: Catholics and education in a changing world*. London: Cassell, 219–41.

Huffington Post (2012) 'Ed Miliband to unveil "One Nation" plan to tackle racial and ethnic segregation'. 14 December. www.huffingtonpost.co.uk/2012/12/14/one-nation-immigration-ed-miliband-labour-ethnic-_n_2298026.html?view=print (accessed 14 December 2012).

Hulmes, E. (1989) *Education and Cultural Diversity*. London: Longmans.

Hurst, J. (2010) 'Religious requirement: The case for Roman Catholic schools in the 1940s and Muslim schools in the 1990s'. *Journal of Beliefs and Values*, 21 (1), 87–97.

Husain, F. and O'Brien, M. (1999) *Muslim Families in Europe: Social existence and social care*. London: University of North London Press.

Husband, C. and Alam, Y. (2011) *Social Cohesion and Counter Terrorism: A policy contradiction*, 1st ed. Bristol: Policy Press.

Hussain, D. (2007) 'Identity formation and change in British Muslim communities'. In M. Wetherell, M. Lafleche, and R. Berkeley (eds), *Identity, Ethnic Diversity and Community Cohesion*. London: Sage.

Hussain, M. (2010) 'Muslim schools: Where faith works'. Online. www.musharrafhussain.com/2012/12/02/muslim-schools-where-faith-works/ (accessed 22 May 2014).

The Independent (2007) 'The grown-ups need to grow up', 18 February: 38.

Independent Review Team (2001) *Community Cohesion: A report of the Independent Review Team chaired by Ted Cantle*. London: Home Office.

The Independent Schools (Employment of Teachers in Schools with a Religious Character) Regulations (2003) Online. www.legislation.gov.uk/uksi/2003/2037/made (accessed 29 June 2014).

Inside Government (2013a) 'Maintained faith schools'. Online. www.gov.uk/government/publications/maintained-faith-schools (accessed 2 June 2013).

—— (2013b) 'Government launches Big Society programme'. Online. www.gov.uk/government/news/government-launches-big-society-programme--2 (accessed 2 June 2013).

Bibliography

ISC (Independent Schools Council) (2014) 'School Regulation and Inspection'. Online. www.isc.co.uk/education-campaigns/campaigns/school-regulation-and-inspection (accessed 12 August 2014).

Jackson, P.I. and Doerschler, P. (2012) *Benchmarking Muslim Well-Being in Europe: Reducing disparities and polarizations.* Bristol: Policy Press.

Jackson, R. (2003) 'Should the State fund faith-based schools? A review of the arguments'. *British Journal of Religious Education*, 25 (2), 89–102.

Jamal, A. and Panjwani, F. (2012) 'Having faith in our schools: Struggling with definitions of religion'. In M. Hunter-Henin (ed.), *Law, Religious Freedoms and Education in Europe.* London: Ashgate.

Janmaat, J.G. (2012) 'The effect of classroom diversity on tolerance and participation in England, Sweden and Germany'. *Journal of Ethnic and Migration Studies*, 38 (1), 21–39.

Jayaweera, H. and Choudhury, T. (2008) *Immigration, faith and cohesion: Evidence from local areas with significant Muslim populations.* York: Joseph Rowntree Foundation.

Jesson, D. (2009) 'Strong schools for strong communities. Reviewing the impact of Church of England schools in promoting community cohesion'. Online. www.churchofengland.org/media/1204726/strong%20schools%20for%20strong%20communities%20-%20cofe%20report%20final.pdf (accessed 20 November 2012).

JLC (Jewish Leadership Council) (2008) *The Future of Jewish Schools. The Commission on Jewish Schools.* London: Jewish Leadership Council. Online. www.thejlc.org/newsite/wp-content/uploads/2011/12/commission.pdf (accessed 1 May 2014).

—— (2010) *New Conceptions of Community.* London: Institute for Jewish Policy Research.

—— (2011) *The Future of Jewish Schools: Three years on – A review of the impact of the Jewish Leadership Council's Commission on Jewish Schools.* London: Jewish Leadership Council.

Jones, N. (2009a) 'Beneath the veil: Muslim girls and Islamic headscarves in secular France'. *Macquarie Law Journal*, 9, 47–69.

—— (2009b) 'Religious freedom in a secular society: The case of the Islamic headscarf in France'. Paper presented at Cultural and Religious Freedom under a Bill of Rights Conference, Canberra, 13–15 August. Online. www.iclrs.org/docs/Religious_freedom_in_a_secular_society_JONES_161109.pdf (accessed 1 May 2014).

Julius, A. (2010) *Trials of the Diaspora: The history of anti-Semitism in England*, 1st ed. Oxford: Oxford University Press.

Kaplan, J. (2013) *Radical Religions and Violence.* London: Routledge.

Karsten, S. (1994) 'Policy on ethnic segregation in a system of choice: The case of the Netherlands'. *Journal of Education Policy*, 9, 211–25.

Keating, A. and Benton, T. (2013) 'Creating cohesive citizens in England? Exploring the role of diversity, deprivation and democratic climate at school'. *Education, Citizenship and Social Justice*, 8 (2), 165–84.

Khattab, N., Johnston, R., Modood, T., and Sirkeci, I. (2011) 'Economic activity in the South-Asian population in Britain: The impact of ethnicity, race and class'. *Ethnic and Racial Studies*, 34 (9), 1466–81.

Kincheloe, J. and Steinberg, S. (1997) *Critical Multiculturalism*. Buckingham: Open University Press.

Knott, K. and McLoughlin, S. (eds) (2010) *Diasporas: Concepts, identities, intersections*. London: Zed Books.

Koenig, J.A. (2011) *Assessing 21st Century Skills: Summary of a workshop*. Washington, DC: National Academies Press.

Kokkonen, A., Esaiasson, P., and Gilljam, M. (2010) 'Ethnic diversity and democratic citizenship: Evidence from a social laboratory'. *Scandinavian Political Studies*, 33 (4), 331–55.

Kressel, N.J. (2007) *Bad Faith: The danger of religious extremism*. New York: Prometheus Books.

Kudani, A. (2002) 'The death of multiculturalism'. *Race & Gender*, 43 (4), 67–72.

Kumar, D. (2012) *Islamophobia and the Politics of Empire*. Chicago: Haymarket Books.

Kymlicka, W. (2012) *Multiculturalism: Success, failure and the future*. Washington, DC: Migration Policy Institute.

Lambert, R. and Githens-Mazer, J. (2010) 'Prevent is dead. What next?'. *The Guardian*. 14 July. Online. www.theguardian.com/commentisfree/belief/2010/jul/14/prevent-counter-radicalisation-terrorism-islam (accessed 19 June 2014).

Lankshear, D.W. (1996) *Churches Serving Schools*. London: The National Society.

—— (2001) 'The relationship between church schools and local church life distinguishing between aided and controlled status'. *Educational Studies*, 27 (4), 425–38.

Lankshear, D.W. and Hall, J.R. (2003) *Governing and Managing Church Schools*. London: The National Society.

Larkin, R.W. (2007) *Comprehending Columbine*. Philadelphia: Temple University Press.

Latour, V. (2012) 'Muscular liberalism: Surviving multiculturalism?: An historical and political contextualisation of David Cameron's Munich speech'. *Observatoire de la Société Britannique*, 12. Online. http://osb.revues.org/1355 (accessed 23 March 2014).

Laurence, J. (2011) 'The effect of ethnic diversity and community disadvantage on social cohesion: A multilevel analysis of social capital and interethnic relations in UK communities'. *European Sociological Review*, 27 (1), 70–89.

Lawton, D. (1980) *The Politics of the School Curriculum*. London: Routledge and Kegan Paul.

Leeman, Y. and Saharson, S. (2013) 'Coming of age in Dutch schools'. *Education*, 4 (1), 11–30.

Lemos, G. and Crane, P. (2005) *The Search for Tolerance: Challenging and changing racist attitudes and behaviour among young people*. York: Joseph Rowntree Foundation.

'Lessons in Hate and Violence', Tazeen Ahmad, reporter. *Dispatches* (Channel 4, 14 February 2011) [television broadcast].

Letki, N. (2008) 'Does diversity erode social cohesion? Social capital and race in British neighbourhoods'. *Political Studies*, 56, 99–126.

Lewis, G. (2004) *Citizenship: Personal lives and social policy*. Milton Keynes: Open University Press.

Bibliography

Lewis, P. (1994) *Islamic Britain: Religion, politics and identity among British Muslims*. London: I.B. Tauris.

Lexilogos (2014) 'Modern Hebrew Dictionary'. Online. www.lexilogos.com/english/hebrew_dictionary.htm (accessed 10 July 2014).

Li, Y., Pickles, A., and Savage, M. (2005) 'Social Capital and Social Trust in Britain in the Late 1990s'. *European Sociological Review*, 21 (1), 109–23.

Liberal Judaism (2012) 'What is liberal Judaism?'. Online. www.liberaljudaism.org/about-us/what-is-liberal-judaism.html (accessed 7 May 2013).

Lijphart, A. (1977) *Democracy in Plural Societies: A comparative exploration*. New Haven, CT: Yale University Press.

Local Government Association (2002) *Guidance on Community Cohesion*. London: Local Government Association.

—— (2002) 'Guidance on community cohesion'. Online. www.tedcantle.co.uk/publications/006%20Guidance%20on%20Community%20Cohesion%20LGA%202002.pdf (accessed 22 May 2014).

—— (2005) *Leading Cohesive Communities: A guide for local authority leaders and chief executives*. London: Local Government Association.

Lynch, J. (1987) *Prejudice Reduction and the Schools*. London: Cassell.

MacEoin, D. (2009) *Music, Chess And Other Sins: Segregation, integration and Muslim schools in Britain*. London: Civitas.

MacMullen, I. (2007) *Faith in Schools?: Autonomy, citizenship, and religious education in the liberal state*. Princeton, NJ: Princeton University Press.

Malik, M. (ed.) (2010) *Patterns of Prejudice: Anti-Muslim prejudice in the West, past and present*. London: Routledge.

Masorti Judaism (2013) 'What is Masorti?'. Online. www.masorti.org.uk/what_is_masorti.htm (accessed 7 May 2013).

McCreery, E., Jones, L., and Holmes, R. (2007) 'Why do Muslim parents want Muslim schools?'. *Early Years*, 27 (3), 203–19.

McGhee, D. (2003) 'Moving to "our" common ground: A critical examination of community cohesion discourse in twenty-first century Britain'. *Sociological Review*, 51 (3), 383–411.

—— (2005) 'Patriots of the future? A critical examination of community cohesion strategies in contemporary Britain'. *Sociological Research Online*, 10 (3). Online. www.socresonline.org.uk/10/3/mcghee.html (accessed 2 June 2013).

McKinney, S.J. (2008) *Faith Schools in the Twenty-First Century*. Edinburgh: Dunedin Academic Press.

McLaughlin, T.H. (1996) 'The distinctiveness of Catholic education'. In T.H. McLaughlin, J. O'Keefe, and B. O'Keefe (eds), *The Contemporary Catholic School: Context, identity and diversity*. London: Falmer Press, 136–54.

Meer, N. and Modood, T. (2009) 'The multicultural state we're in: Muslims, multiculture and the "civic rebalancing" of British multiculturalism'. *Political Studies*, 57 (3), 473–97.

—— (2011) 'Framing contemporary citizenship and diversity in Europe'. In T. Modood, A. Triandafyllidou, and R. Zapata-Barrero (eds), *Multiculturalism, Muslims and Citizenship: A European approach*. London: Routledge.

—— (2012) 'How does interculturalism contrast with multiculturalism?'. *Journal of Intercultural Studies*, 33 (2), 175–96.

Meer, N., Dwyer, C., and Modood, T. (2010) 'Embodying nationhood? Conceptions of British national identity, citizenship and gender in the "Veil Affair"'. *The Sociological Review*, 58 (1), 84–111.

Merriam, S.B. (2009) *Qualitative Research: A guide to design and implementation*. San Francisco: Jossey-Bass.

Miller, H. (2007) *Accountability Through Inspection: Monitoring and evaluating Jewish schools*. London: Board of Deputies of British Jews.

—— (2011) *Four Years On: A review of inspections of Jewish schools 2007–2011*. London: Board of Deputies of British Jews.

Miller, H., Grant, L.D., and Pomson, A. (2011) *International Handbook of Jewish Education*. New York: Springer Science Business Media.

Ministère des Affaires Étrangères (2007) 'Secularism in France'. Online. www.ambafrance-pk.org/IMG/pdf/secularism.pdf (accessed 22 March 2014).

Modood, J.M. (2009) 'Religious education and citizenship'. In A. Elliot and H. Poon (eds), *Growing Citizens: An interdisciplinary reflection on citizenship education*. Edinburgh: St Andrews Press.

Modood, T. (1998) 'Racial equality: Colour, culture and justice'. In D. Boucher and P.J. Kelly (eds), *Perspectives on Social Justice: From Hume to Walzer*. London: Routledge, 203–17.

—— (2003) 'Muslims and European multiculturalism'. *Open Democracy*. Online. www.opendemocracy.net/faith-europe_islam/article_1214.jsp (accessed 19 May 2014).

—— (2005) *Multicultural Politics: Racism, ethnicity and Muslims in Britain*. Edinburgh: Edinburgh University Press.

—— (2007) *Multiculturalism: A civic idea*. Cambridge: Polity.

—— (2008) *Multiculturalism after 7/7: A scapegoat or a hope for the future?: The RUSI Journal*, 153 (2), 14–17.

—— (2009) 'Ethnicity and religion'. In M. Flinders, A. Gamble, C. Hay, and M. Kenny (eds), *Oxford Handbook of British Politics*. Oxford: Oxford University Press.

—— (2010) *Still Not Easy Being British: Struggles for a multicultural citizenship*. Stoke-on-Trent: Trentham Books.

—— (2013) *Multiculturalism*, 2nd ed. Cambridge: Polity Press.

Modood, T. and Ahmed, F. (2007) 'British Muslim perspectives on multiculturalism'. *Theory, Culture and Society*, 24 (2), 187–212.

Modood, T., Beishon, S., and Virdee, S. (1994) *Changing Ethnic Identities*. London: Policy Studies Institute.

Modood, T. and Dobbernack, J. (2011) 'A left communitarianism? What about multiculturalism?'. *Soundings*, 48 (Summer), 54–65.

Modood, T. and Kastoryano, R. (2006) 'Secularism and the accommodation of Muslims in Europe'. In T. Modood, A. Triandafyllidou, R. and Zapata-Barrero, R. (eds), *Multiculturalism, Muslims and Citizenship: A European approach*. London: Routledge.

Modood, T. and Werbner, P. (1997) *The Politics of Multiculturalism in the New Europe: Racism, identity and community*. London: Zed Books.

Montessori, M. (1964) *The Montessori Method*. New York: Random House.

Bibliography

Mookerjee, M. (2005) 'Affective Citizenship: Feminism, postcolonialism and the politics of recognition'. *Critical Review of International Social and Political Philosophy*, 8 (1), 31–50.

Morris, A. (2012) 'Faith schools and the plural society: Exploring notions of diversity in school provision in England'. *Policy Futures in Education*, 10 (5), 518–27.

Muir, H., Smith, L. and Richardson, R. (2004) *Islamophobia: Issues, challenges and action – A report by the Commission on British Muslims and Islamophobia*. Stoke-on-Trent: Trentham Books.

Murray, G. (2006) 'France: The riots and the Republic'. *Race and Class*, 47 (4), 26–45.

Muslim Directory (2014) 'Islamic Education in South Africa'. Online. www.muslim.co.za (accessed 6 April 2014).

National Society (2003) *Governing and Managing Church Schools*. London: The National Society.

Nielsen, J.S. (2004) *Muslims in Europe*, 3rd ed. Edinburgh: Edinburgh University Press.

—— (2009) 'Religion, Muslims and the state in Britain and France: From Westphalia to 9/11'. In A.H. Sinno (ed.), *Muslims in Western Politics*. Bloomington: Indiana University Press, 50–69.

O'Keefe, B. (1997) 'The changing role of Catholic schools in England and Wales: From exclusiveness to engagement'. In J. McMahon, H. Neidharty, and J. Chapman (eds), *Leading the Catholic School*. Richmond, Victoria: Spectrum.

—— (1999) 'Reordering perspectives in Catholic schools'. In M. Hornsby-Smith (ed.), *Catholics in England 1950–2000*. London: Cassell.

—— (2000) 'Fidelity and openness: A Christian response to pluralism'. *International Journal of Education and Religion*. 1 (1), 122–34.

O'Toole, T., Nilsson DeHanas, D., and Modood, T. (2012) 'Balancing tolerance, security and Muslim engagement in the United Kingdom: The impact of the "Prevent" agenda'. *Critical Studies on Terrorism*, 5 (3), 373–89.

OECD (Organisation for Economic Cooperation and Development) (2006) *Annual Report*. Online. www.oecd.org/newsroom/36511265.pdf (accessed 19 May 2014).

—— (n.d.) 'Programme for International Student Assessment (PISA)'. Online. www.oecd.org/pisa (accessed 24 February 2014).

Office of National Statistics (2011) *Focus on Ethnicity and Religion*. Basingstoke: Palgrave Macmillan.

Ofsted (2009) 'Independent faith schools'. Online. www.ofsted.gov.uk/resources/independent-faith-schools (accessed 27 February 2014).

—— (2011) 'Islamic Montessori school'. Online. www.ofsted.gov.uk/inspection-reports (accessed 12 June 2013).

—— (2013) 'The Framework for School Inspection'. Online. www.ofsted.gov.uk/resources/framework-for-school-inspection (accessed 22 March 2014).

Oliver, J.E. and Mandelberg, T. (2000) 'Reconsidering the environmental determinants of white racial attitudes'. *American Journal of Political Science*, 44 (3), 574–89.

Osler, A. and Starkey, H. (2005) *Changing Citizenship: Democracy and inclusion in education*. Maidenhead: Open University Press.

Ouseley, H. (2001) *Community Pride and Prejudice: Making diversity work in Bradford*. Bradford: Bradford City Council. Online. http://resources.cohesioninstitute.org.uk/Publications/Documents/Document/Default.aspx?recordId=98 (accessed 1 May 2014).

Panjwani, F. (2012) 'Why did you not tell me about this? Religion as a challenge to faith schools'. In H. Alexander and A. Agbaria (eds), *Commitment, Character, and Citizenship: Religious education in liberal democracy*. New York: Routledge.

Parekh, B. (2000) *Rethinking Multiculturalism: Cultural diversity and political theory*. Basingstoke: Macmillan.

—— (2002a) 'Common belonging'. In Runnymede Trust (ed.), *Cohesion, Community and Citizenship: Proceedings of a Runnymede conference*. London: Runnymede Trust.

—— (2002b) 'Dilemmas of a multicultural theory of citizenship'. *Constellations*, 4 (1), 54–62.

Parker-Jenkins, M. (1995) *Children of Islam: A teacher's guide to meeting the educational needs of Muslim children*. Stoke-on-Trent: Trentham Books.

—— (2002) 'Equal access to state funding: The case of Muslim schools in Britain'. *Race, Ethnicity and Education*, 5 (3), 273–89.

—— (2008) *Terms of Engagement: Muslim and Jewish school communities, cultural sustainability and maintenance of religious identity*. ESRC Full Research Report, RES-000-22-2218. Swindon: ESRC. [Full research by Marie Parker-Jenkins and Meli Glenn.] Online. www.esrc.ac.uk/my-esrc/grants/RES-000-22-2218/outputs/Read/01be7703-6c25-4b91-a400-df26e505f290 (accessed 29 April 2014).

—— (2011) 'Children's rights and wrongs: Lessons from Strasbourg'. *International Journal of Law and Education*, 16 (1), 87–106.

Parker-Jenkins, M. and Glenn, M. (2011) 'Levels of community cohesion: Theorizing the UK agenda on promoting cohesion and the implications for faith-based schools'. *International Journal of Multicultural Education*, 13 (1). Online. www.ijme-journal.org/index.php/ijme/article/view/323 (accessed 28 April 2013).

Parker-Jenkins, M., Hartas, D., and Irving, B. (2005) *In Good Faith: Schools, religion and public funding*. London: Ashgate.

Parker-Jenkins, M., Hewitt, D., Brownhill, S., and Sanders, T. (2007) *Aiming High: Strategies to raise the attainment of pupils from culturally diverse backgrounds*. London: Sage.

Parsons, G. (1994) *The Growth of Religious Diversity: Britain from 1945*. 2 vols. London: Routledge, for the Open University.

Peach, C. (2005) 'Britain's Muslim population: An overview' and 'Muslims in the UK'. In T. Abbas (ed.), *Muslim Britain: Communities under pressure*. London: Zed Books.

Pearce, J. (2004) *Background of Distances, Participation and Community Cohesion in the North: Making the connections*. Bradford: International Centre for Participation Studies, University of Bradford.

Pearce, S. (2005) *You Wouldn't Understand: White teachers in multiethnic classrooms*. Stoke-on-Trent: Trentham Books.

Bibliography

Pellegrino, J.W. and Hilton, M. (2012) *Education for Life and Work: Developing transferable knowledge and skills in the 21st century*. Washington, DC: National Academies Press.

Peters, M.A. and Besley, T. (2014) 'Islam and the end of European multiculturalism? From multiculturalism to civic integration'. *Policy Futures in Education*, 12 (1). Online. www.wwwords.co.uk/pdf/validate.asp?j=pfie&vol=12&issue=1&year=2014&article=1_Editorial_PFIE_12_1_web (accessed 22 May 2014).

Pettigrew, T.F. and Tropp, L.R. (2006) 'A meta-analytic test of inter-group contact theory'. *Journal of Personality and Social Psychology*, 90 (5), 751–83.

Pettinger, P. (2012) 'The evidence base on the effects of policy and practice in faith schools'. *Forum: For promoting 3-19 comprehensive education*, 54 (1), 113–23.

Phillips, D. (2006) 'Parallel lives? Challenging discourses of British Muslim self segregation'. *Environment and Planning D: Society and Space*, 24 (1), 25–40.

Phillips, M. (2005) 'This lethal moral madness'. *Daily Mail*, 14 July. Online. www.dailymail.co.uk/debate/columnists/article-355770/This-lethal-moral-madness.html (accessed 27 August 2013).

Pikuach (2009) *Revised Framework*. London: Board of Deputies of British Jews.

Pring, R. (2005) 'Are faith schools justified?'. In R. Gardner, J. Cairns, and D. Lawton (eds), *Faith Schools: Consensus or conflict?*. London: RoutledgeFalmer.

—— (2012) 'Common school or common system?'. In M. Shuayb (ed.), *Rethinking Education for Social Cohesion*. Basingstoke: Palgrave.

Pugh, G. and Telhaj, S. (2007) 'Faith schools, social capital and academic attainment: Evidence from TIMSS-R mathematics scores in Flemish secondary schools'. *British Educational Research Journal*, 32 (2), 235–67.

Putnam, R.D. (2002) *Democracies in Flux: The evolution of social capital in contemporary society*. Oxford: Oxford University Press.

QCA (2004) 'The national framework for religious education'. Online. www.qca.org.uk (accessed 1 June 2008).

Qureshi, S. and Khan, J. (1989) *The Politics of Satanic Verses: Unmasking western attitudes*. Leicester: Muslim Communities Studies Institute.

Race, A. and Hedges, P.M. (eds) (2008) *Christian Approaches to Other Faiths*. London: SCM Press.

Race Relations Act 1976 (Amendment) Regulations (2003) Online. www.legislation.gov.uk/uksi/2003/1626/contents/made (accessed 22 May 2014).

Race Relations (Amendment) Act (2000) Online. www.legislation.gov.uk/ukpga/2000/34/contents (accessed 22 May 2014).

Rattansi, A. (ed.) (1992) *Race, Culture and Difference*. London: Sage.

Reform Judaism (2013) 'What is Reform Judaism?'. Online. www.reformjudaism.org.uk/about-us/what-is-reform-judaism.html (accessed 7 May 2013).

Rex, J. (1970) *Race Relations in Sociological Theory*. New York: Schoken Books.

Richardson, R. (2009) *Islamophobia or Anti-Muslim Racism – or What?: Concepts and terms revisited*. London: Insted. Online. www.insted.co.uk/anti-muslim-racism.pdf (accessed 27 February 2014).

Richardson, R. and Wood, A. (2004) *The Achievement of British Pakistani Learners: Work in progress* (The report of the RAISE Project 2002–4, funded by Yorkshire Forward). Stoke-on-Trent: Trentham Books.

Riley, K. and Louis, K. (2004) *Exploring New Forms of Community Leadership: Linking schools and communities to improve educational opportunities for young people*. Nottingham: National College for School Leadership.

Rizvi, S. (2008) 'Ethnographic research in a Muslim school: Reflections on fieldwork experience'. In D. Sridhar (ed.), *Anthropologists Inside Organizations: South Asian case studies*. New Delhi: Sage.

—— (2010) 'Telling the whole story: An anthropological conversation on conflicting discourses of integration, identity, and socialization'. In R. Acosta, S. Rizvi and A. Santos (eds), *Making Sense of the Global: Anthropological perspectives on interconnections and processes*. Newcastle-upon-Tyne: Cambridge Scholars.

Roelsma-Somer, S. (2008) 'De kwaliteit van hindoescholen. [The quality of Hindu schools]'. Unpublished PhD thesis, University of Tilburg.

Romain, J. (1985) *The Jews of England*. London: Michael Goulston Educational Foundation.

Ross, C.E., Mirowsky, J., and Pribesh, S. (2001) 'Powerlessness and the amplification of threat: Neighborhood disadvantage, disorder, and mistrust'. *American Sociological Review*, 66 (4), 568–91.

Roth, W-M. (2006) 'Contradictions in theorizing and implementing communities in education'. *Education Research Review*, 1, 27–40.

Rowe, D., Horsley, N., Thorpe, T., and Breslin, T. (2011) 'School leaders, community cohesion and the Big Society'. Reading: CfBT Education Trust. Online. http://cdn.cfbt.com/~/media/cfbtcorporate/files/research/2011/r-community-cohesion-perspective-2011.pdf (accessed 9 February 2014).

Rowe, D. and Horsley, N. with Thorpe, T. and Breslin, T. (2013) *A Study of Primary and Secondary Schools' Responses to a New Statutory Duty*. Reading: CFBT Education Trust.

Runnymede Trust (1994) *A Very Light Sleeper: The persistence and dangers of antisemitism*. London: Runnymede Trust.

—— (1997) *Islamophobia: A challenge for us all*. London: Runnymede Trust.

—— (2007) *Islamophobia*. London: Runnymede Trust.

Sacks, J. (2000) *The Politics of Hope*. London: Vintage.

—— (2002) *The Dignity of Difference: How to avoid the clash of civilizations*. London: Continuum.

—— (2007) *The Home We Build Together: Recreating society*. London: Continuum.

Said, E. (1978) *Orientalism: Western representations of the Orient*. New York: Vintage.

—— (2003) *Orientalism*. London: Penguin.

Sarwar, G. (1992) *Islam: Beliefs and teachings*, 4th ed. London: Muslim Educational Trust.

Schagen, I. and Schagen, S. (2005) 'Combining multilevel analysis with national value-added data sets: A case study to explore the effects of school diversity'. *British Educational Research Journal*, 31 (3), 309–28.

Schagen, S., Davies, D., Rudd, P., and Schagen, I. (2002) *The Impact of Specialist and Faith Schools on Performance (LGA Research Report 28)*. Slough: NFER.

Bibliography

Schlesinger, E. (2003) *Creating Community and Accumulating Social Capital: Jews associating with other Jews in Manchester*. London: Institute for Jewish Policy Research.

Schmool, M. and Cohen, F. (1998) *A Profile of British Jewry*. London: Board of Deputies of British Jews.

School Standards and Framework Act (1998) Online. www.legislation.gov.uk/ukpga/1998/31/contents (accessed 22 May 2014).

Scott, S. and McNeish, D. (2012) *Leadership and Faith Schools: Issues and challenges*. Nottingham: National College for School Leadership.

Seddon, M.S. and Ahmad, F. (2012) *Muslim Youth: Challenges, opportunities and expectations*. London: Continuum.

Shah, S. (2012) 'Muslim schools in secular societies: Persistence or resistance!'. *British Journal of Religious Education*, 34 (1), 51–65.

Shain, F. (2011) *The New Folk Devils: Muslim boys and education in England*. Stoke-on-Trent: Trentham Books.

Shanneil, Y. (2011) 'Conversion and religious habitus: The experiences of Irish women converts to Islam in the pre-Celtic Tiger era'. *Journal of Muslim Minority Affairs*, 31 (4), 503–17.

Shaw, A. (1988) *A Pakistani Community in Britain*. Oxford: Basil Blackwell.

Shome, R. (2012) 'Mapping the limits of multiculturalism in the context of globalisation'. *International Journal of Communications*, 6, 144–65.

Short, G. (2002) 'Faith-based schools: A threat to social cohesion?'. *Journal of Philosophy of Education*, 36 (4), 559–72.

—— (2003) 'Faith schools and social cohesion: Opening up the debate'. *British Journal of Educational Studies*, 25 (2), 129–41.

Short, G. and Lenga, R. (2002) 'Faith schools and social cohesion: Opening up the debate'. *British Journal of Beliefs and Values*, 25 (1), 43–54.

Shuayb, M. (2012) 'Current models and approaches to social cohesion in secondary schools in Lebanon'. In M. Shuayb (ed.), *Rethinking Education for Social Cohesion*. Basingstoke: Palgrave.

Smithers, R. (2005) 'Anger at Muslim schools attack: Claims by education chief "derogatory"'. *The Guardian*, 18 January. Online. www.theguardian.com/uk/2005/jan/18/schools.faithschools (accessed 1 May 2014).

Spanish and Portuguese Jews' Congregation (2013) 'History'. Online. www.sandp.org/history.html (accessed 7 May 2013).

Statham, J., Harris, A., and Glenn, M. (2010) *Strengthening Family Well-being and Community Cohesion Through the Role of Schools and Extended Services*. London: Centre for Excellence and Outcomes in Children and Young People's Services.

Steiner, R. (1966) *Study of Man: General education course: Fourteen lectures given in Stuttgart, 21st August–5th September 1919*. Dornach, Switzerland: Rudolf Steiner Press.

Stern, J. (2006) *Teaching Religious Education*. London: Continuum.

Steyn, M. (2005) 'A victory for multiculturalism over common sense'. *Daily Telegraph*, 12 February.

Suto, I. (2013) *21st Century Skills: Ancient, ubiquitous, enigmatic?*. Cambridge: Cambridge University Press.

Taylor, M. (2006) 'It's official: Class matters'. *The Guardian*, 28 February. Online. www.theguardian.com/education/2006/feb/28/schools.education (accessed 29 April 2014).

Taylor, P., Richardson, J., Yeo, A., Marsh, I., Trobe, K., Pilkington, K., Hughes, G., and Sharp, K. (2002) *Sociology in Focus*. Ormskirk: Causeway Press.

Thobani, S. (2010) *Islam in the School Curriculum: Symbolic pedagogy and cultural claims*. London: Continuum.

—— (2011) 'Pedagogic discourses and imagined communities: Knowing Islam and being Muslim'. *Discourse: Studies in the Cultural Politics of Education*, 32 (4), 531–45.

Thomas, E.R. (2012) *Immigration, Islam and the Politics of Belonging in France: A comparative framework*. Philadelphia: University of Pennsylvania Press.

Times Educational Supplement (2001) 'Faith schools: Opposition multiplies', 5 October: 1.

Tinker, C. (2006) 'State Funded Muslim schools?: Equality, identity and community in multifaith Britain'. Unpublished PhD thesis, Nottingham University.

Tony Blair Faith Foundation (n.d.) Online. www.tonyblairfaithfoundation.org/ (accessed 22 February 2014).

Toynbee, P. (2001) 'Keep God out of class'. *The Guardian*, 9 November. Online. www.theguardian.com/education/2001/nov/09/schools.uk (accessed 1 May 2014).

Triandafyllidou, A. (2011) *Addressing Cultural, Ethnic & Religious Diversity Challenges in Europe: A comparative overview of 15 European countries*. Florence: European University Institute.

—— (2012) *Handbook on Tolerance and Cultural Diversity in Europe*. Florence: European University Institute.

Tropp, A. (1957) *The School Teachers: The growth of the teaching profession in England and Wales from 1800 to the present day*. London: Heinemann.

Troyna, B. and Carrington, B. (1990) *Education, Racism and Reform*. London: Routledge.

UK Action Committee on Islamic Affairs (1993) *Muslims and the Law in Multi Faith Britain: The need for reform*. London: UK Action Committee on Islamic Affairs.

The United Synagogue (n.d.) 'Welcome to the United Synagogue'. Online. www.theus.org.uk/the_united_synagogue/about_the_us/welcome/ (accessed 7 May 2013).

Valins, O. (2003) 'Defending identities or segregating communities? Faith-based schooling and the UK Jewish community'. *Geoforum*, 34 (2), 235–47.

Valins, O., Kosmin, B., and Goldberg, J. (2001) *The Future of Jewish Schooling in the United Kingdom: A strategic assessment of a faith-based provision of primary and secondary school education (planning for Jewish communities)*. London: Institute for Jewish Policy Research.

Varshney, A. (2002) *Ethnic Conflict and Civic Life: Hindus and Muslims in India*. New Haven, CT: Yale University Press.

Veinguer, A.A., Dietz, G., Joza, D.P., and Knauth, T. (2009) *Islam in Education in Europe: Pedagogical concepts and empirical findings*. New York: Waxmann.

Bibliography

Vermeulen, B.P. (2004) 'Regulating school choice to promote civic values: Constitutional and political issues in the Netherlands'. In P.J. Wolf. and S. Macedo (eds), *Educating Citizens: International perspectives on civic values and school choice*. Washington, D.C.: Brookings Institution Press.

Vertovec, S. (2002) 'Islamophobia and Muslim recognition in Britain'. In Y.Y. Haddad (ed.), *Muslims in the West: From sojourners to citizens*. Oxford: Oxford University Press.

Vogt, W.P. (1997) *Tolerance and Education: Learning to live with diversity and difference*. Thousand Oaks, CA: Sage.

Walford, G. (1991) *Private Schooling: Tradition, change and diversity*. London: Paul Chapman.

—— (2000) 'Funding for private schools in England and the Netherlands: Can the piper call the tune?' Occasional Paper No. 8. New York: National Center for the Study of Privatization in Education. Online. www.ncspe.org/publications_files/209_OP08.pdf (accessed 22 May 2014).

—— (2001) 'Funding for religious schooling in England and the Netherlands: Can the piper call the tune?'. *Research Papers in Education*, 16 (4), 359–80.

—— (2002) 'Classification and framing of the curriculum in evangelical and Muslim schools in England and the Netherlands'. *Educational Studies*, 28 (4), 403–19.

—— (2003) *British Private Schools: Research on policy and practice*. London: Woburn.

Wardle, D. (1976) *English Popular Education 1780–1975*, 2nd ed. Cambridge: Cambridge University Press.

Webber, R. and Butler, T. (2005) 'Classifying pupils by where they live: How well does this predict variations in their GCSE results?' (CASA Working Paper Series). London: Centre for Advanced Spatial Analysis, University College London.

Weekes-Bernard, D. (2007) *School Choice and Ethnic Segregation: Educational disadvantage decision-making among black and minority ethnic parents*. London: Runnymede Trust.

Weller, P. (2005) 'Religions and social capital: Theses on religion(s), state(s), and society(ies), with particular reference to the UK and the European Union'. *Journal of International Migration and Integration*, 6 (2), 271–89.

—— (2011) *Religious Discrimination in Britain: A review of research evidence, 2000–10*. Manchester: Equality and Human Rights Commission.

Weller, P., Feldman, A., and Purdam, K. (with contributions from Andrews, A., Doswell, A., Hinnells, J., Parker-Jenkins, M., Parmar, S., and Wolfe, M.) (2001) *Religious Discrimination in England and Wales*. Home Office Research Study 220. London: Research, Development and Statistics Directorate, The Home Office.

Wellington, J. (2000) *Educational Research: Contemporary issues and practical approaches*. London: Continuum.

Werbner, P. (2001) 'The vulnerabilities of the Muslim population in Britain'. *Times Higher Education Supplement*, 14 December: 30–1.

—— (2002) *The Migrant Process: Capital: gifts and offerings among Manchester Pakistanis*. Oxford: Berg.

—— (2009) 'Revisiting the UK Muslim diasporic public sphere at a time of terror'. *South Asian Diaspora*, 1 (1), 14–45.

—— (2012) 'Folk devils and racist imaginaries in a global prism: Islamophobia and anti-Semitism in the twenty-first century'. *Ethnic and Racial Studies*, 36 (3), 450–67.

West-Burnham, J., Farrar, M., and Otero, G. (2007) *Schools and Communities: Working together to transform children's lives*. New York: Network Continuum.

Wetherell, M., Lafleche, M., and Berkeley, R. (2007) *Identity, Ethnic Diversity and Community Cohesion*. London: Sage.

Woodhead, L. (2011) 'Recent research on religion, discrimination, and good relations. EHRC Research Report no. 48'. Manchester: Equality and Human Rights Commission. Online. www.religionandsociety.org.uk/uploads/docs/2011_05/1306247842_LINDA_WOODHEAD_FINAL_REPORT_MAY_2011.pdf (accessed 10 June 2013).

Worley, C (2005) '"It's not about race. It's about community": New Labour and community cohesion'. *Critical Social Policy*, 25 (4), 483–96.

Wright, F. (2003) 'Integrated education in Northern Ireland: Its history, impact on students, and role in the peacebuilding process'. Online. www.pur.honorscollege.pitt.edu/docs/v22n1-integrated-education-burchill.pdf (accessed 12 August 2014).

Yeshanew, T., Schagen, I., and Evans, S. (2008) 'Faith schools and pupils' progress through primary education'. *Educational Studies*, 34 (5), 511–26.

Yin, R.K. (2009) *Case Study Research: Design and methods*, 4th ed. London: Sage.

Young, J. (2003) 'To these wet and windy shores: Recent immigration policy in the UK'. *Punishment & Society*, 40 (5), 449–62.

Yuval-Davis, N. (2009) 'Interview with Professor Nira Yuval-Davis: After gender and nation'. Interview by Lois Lee. *Studies in Ethnicity and Nationalism*, 9 (1), 128–38.

Zebri, K. (2008) *British Muslim Converts: Choosing alternative lives*. Oxford: Oneworld.

Zine, J. (2008) *Canadian Islamic Schools: Unravelling the politics of gender, knowledge and identity*. Toronto: University of Toronto Press.

Index

Abdul-Rahman, S.M.   67
Akhtar, S.   37
Alibhai-Brown, Y.   40, 100
alienation, and community engagement   13, 42
Allen, C.   75
Anglican schooling   17, 23; and openness   36
anti-Semitism   23, 96, 97, 106; and bullying   56–3; definition   4
Apple, M.   93
Ashkenazi Jews   23, 52
Ashraf, S.A.   72
assessment programmes: Face to Faith   94; PISA   93; *see also* skill development
assimilation: and fear   10, 13, 80; and integration   107, 109; and multiculturalism   98–102; promotion of   13, 30
associational engagement   88

Bald, J.   15, 108
Barber, M.   83, 90, 92–3
Belgium, openness of Catholic schools   38
Bell, D.   40
Berkeley, R.   9, 13, 15, 73, 89, 107–8
Big Society   5, 13, 14, 41, 96, 98, 111
bonding   7, 15, 32, 46, 67, 86, 89
British and Foreign School Society   18
'Britishness', and multiculturalism   14, 42, 99, 101–2
Bruce, S.   26
Bryk, A.   36
bullying: and anti-Semitism   56–3; Muslim   73, 80–1
Burgess, S.   8, 10
Burnett, J.   42, 43

Cameron, D.   41, 110
Cantle, T.   7, 45, 99, 106
Cantle report   35, 40, 42, 100
Carr, J.   75, 76
Catholic schools   23, 25; in England and Wales   18–19, 34; in France   30; in the Netherlands   28–9; in Northern Ireland   27–8; openness of   37–8; in Scotland   26–7; and sectarianism   45–6
Central Orthodoxy   52
Charedi Judaism   52
charity, and engagement   73, 85, 87, 105
Cheong, P.H.   40, 100
Children's Plan, The (DCSF)   14
Choudhury, T.   46, 47, 78

citizenship education: and community engagement   13; and curricula   101, 108; government policies   39–40, 52; and multiculturalism   99, 103, 107
clothing: *hijab*   30–1, 68–9, 78, 80–1; Jewish   51
COIC (Commission on Integration and Cohesion)   40–1
Coleman, J.S.   7, 66
community cohesion: and Big Society   5, 13, 14, 41, 96, 98, 111; definitions   12–13, 40, 41; and engagement   55, 59, 81, 98, 105, 107–9; and integration   41–7, 110; Jewish   50, 54–6, 59; Muslim   67, 81; policies   39–42, 105–6; and trust   12, 38, 43, 76, 107; *see also* engagement
community engagement *see* engagement
competition (school), and parental choice   9, 10, 15
Conroy, J.C.   26
Creechurch Lane Talmud Torah School   22
CRP (Certificate of Religious Practice)   51
CTCs (City Technology Colleges)   25
curriculum: adaptation to national standards   25, 47, 67, 71; and citizenship education   101, 108; and cohesion   15, 58; and engagement   72–3, 81, 98; and Jewish ethos   51; models of skill development   90–3

Dar ul-Uloom schools   2, 24, 65, 70
Dawkins, R.   15, 34, 89
DCSF (Department for Children, Schools and Families)   12, 14, 41, 50, 81, 83, 105, 109
Deer, C.   30
Denham, J.   3, 5, 58
denominational schools   11, 23, 27, 29; origins   17–19
deprivation, and diversity   41, 43–5
Devine, D.   77, 98, 106
DFE (Department for Education)   9, 14, 24, 25, 42, 51, 52, 75, 100, 103, 108, 109
DfEE (Department for Education and Employment)   11, 25
DfES (Department for Education and Skills)   21
Dijkstra, A.B.   36
discrimination: debates on   34–9; and legislation   101, 104; Muslims'   76; and teachers' employment   22; *see also* bullying
diversity: and cohesion   10, 12, 40–1, 100; and deprivation   41, 43–5; within Jewish community   23, 52–4; within Muslim community   2, 24–5, 65, 70–2, 81; and tolerance   37
division   28, 34, 42, 44–5; *see also* sectarianism; segregation
Dronkers, S.   9, 10
Dutch Reformed Church   29
Dyson, A.   87

Education Act (1944)   11, 19, 21, 24
Education Act (1996)   20–1

137

Education Act (2002) 14, 40, 88
Education and Inspections Act (2006) 9, 21, 41, 81
Education Reform Act (1988) 8, 11
Elchardus, M. 38
Elementary Education Act (1870) 11
Elementary School Act (1870) 19
engagement: associational 88; and charity activities 73, 105; and community cohesion 55, 59, 81, 98, 105, 107–9; definition 13–14, 83; and hostility 47, 71, 76, 85; in Jewish schools 86; levels of 87–8; and Muslim identity 71–3; policies for development 93–5; promotion of 84, 98; skill development models 88–93; and trust 84–5
England: history of religious schools 17–19; openness of Anglican schools 36; origins of Jewish education 22; origins of Muslim education 23; types of faith schools 24–5
ethnicity: and identity 7–8, 104; and integration 41–7, 99–100, 103, 107–9; and segregation 34–6; *see also* discrimination; diversity
ethos: and engagement 65–6, 71–3, 84, 89, 98; and gender separation 51; and parental choice 11, 15
European Convention on Human Rights 9
European Monitoring Centre on Racism and Xenophobia 4, 5, 56, 57
Everett, H. 34, 36, 38, 46
exclusion 38, 39, 43, 44–5, 101, 102; self-exclusion 3, 23, 58; *see also* discrimination; isolation; segregation
exclusivism 35–6, 45

Face to Faith programme 94
fear: and alienation 13; of assimilation 80, 99–100; and diversity 59, 61–2, 73, 74–5
Finney, N. 68–9, 74, 81, 92, 99, 102, 106, 109–10
Flint, J. 40, 42, 45
Florida, R. 92
France, and secularism 29–32, 69
Francis, L.J. 19, 109
fundamentalism 7, 25, 35, 43, 76, 79, 99
funding: independent schools 11, 20–1, 24–6, 46–7, 51, 54, 56, 66, 85; state-funded schools 15, 18–19, 21, 23, 25, 27, 29, 33–4, 49, 50–1, 66
Furbey, R. 84, 94
Future of Jewish Schools, The 11

Gaine, C. 13, 87
Gates of Hope School 22
gender: and dress code 30–1, 68–9; separation 51
Gibbons, S. 9, 10
Gilby, N. 70
Glenn, M. 67, 106
Gove, M. 41–2, 100

Grace, G. 18, 35, 36, 45
Graham, D. 51, 52
Greeley, A. 37, 38
Guidance on the Duty to Promote Community Cohesion (DCSF) 12, 41

halacha 52
Halstead, J.M. 20, 28, 34, 36, 65, 66, 67, 70, 79
Haneef, S. 67
Harrison, M. 42
Haynes, A. 75, 76
headscarf *see hijab*
Hewer, C. 11, 25, 67, 70, 80
Hick, J. 35
hijab: and bullying 78, 80–1; and dress code 68–9; and French secularism 30–1, 69
Hilton, M. 90
Home Office 5, 100; *Citizenship Survey* 44; community cohesion definition 40
Hopkins, N. 108
hostility: and engagement 47, 71–3, 85; and segregation 34–5, 46–7, 97; *see also* anti-Semitism; fear; Islamophobia
Hulmes, E. 8, 72
Hurst, J. 46

identity: and ethnicity 7–8, 104; Jewish 8, 53–5, 59, 108; Muslim 67–8, 70–3, 76–7, 104; sectarian 34; and tolerance 20, 36–7; *see also* multiculturalism
ideological neutrality 33
imam 66
inclusivism, religious 35–6
independent schools 11, 20–1, 24–6, 46–7, 51, 54, 56, 66, 85; *see also* state-funded schools
inspection 21, 51; and community cohesion 41–2, 70, 97, 99; Pikuach reports 24, 53, 86
integration: and assimilation 107–9; and community cohesion 41–7, 110; and multiculturalism 99–100, 103, 105
interculturalism 37, 94, 104–5
intolerance *see* tolerance
IPDJS (Institute of Professional Development for Jewish Schools) 52
Islamophobia 3, 6, 97, 106; and bullying 73, 80–1; definitions 4–5, 75; and hostility 23–4, 46, 59–60, 72; and security 74–5, 77–9; *see also* xenophobia

Jackson, P.I. 20, 81
Janmaat, J.G. 37
Jewish Educators Network 52
Jewish Free School 50–1
Jewish Leadership Council 11

138

Index

Jewish schooling: and community cohesion 54–6; diversity within 23, 52–4; and engagement initiatives 86; features 50–2; inspection services 24, 53, 86; origins in England 22; parental choice 11; policies 49–50; and security 56, 57, 59–62
Jones, N. 30–1, 69
Julius, A. 57

Kavadias, D. 38
Khattab, N. 102
kippah 51
Koenig, J.A. 91–2
Kudani, A. 6, 7, 8
Kumar, D. 75, 76

Labour Party, promotion of cohesion 9, 10, 39–40, 42, 46, 71, 100, 105–6
laicism, French 31
leadership: development models 91–2; religious 65–6, 70
Lebanon, and social cohesion 38
Letki, N. 44, 109
Liberal Judaism 53

MacMullen, I. 7, 106
Madrassah 4, 46–7, 66
Mandelberg, T. 43
Masorti Judaism 52–3
McGhee, D. 45
McLaughlin, T.H. 20, 28, 34, 35, 36, 66
Meer, N. 103, 104–5
Miller, H. 8, 11, 19, 49, 84, 86, 87–8, 94, 106, 107, 111
Modood, T. 66, 78, 80, 81, 101–2, 103, 104–5
Muir, H. 75
multiculturalism 6–7, 33–4; and cohesion 14, 42, 86, 99–100, 106, 111; discourse on 39–40, 68, 103–4; and interculturalism 104–5; policies 101–2, 105–6, 108–9
Muslim schooling: and clothing 68–9; diversity within 2, 24–5, 65, 70–2, 81; faith leaders 66; and identity 67–8, 70–3, 104; origins in England 23; and parental choice 11; and security 69–70, 76–7; and segregation 46–7

NAJOS (National Association of Jewish Orthodox Schools) 50
National Schools 18
neighbourhood socio-economic status (SES) 43–4
Netherlands, The 28–9; openness of faith schools 36
neutrality, ideological 33
Nielsen, J.S. 24, 31, 67
Northern Ireland 27–8, 35
NVivo software 3

Ofsted (Office for Standards in Education) 10, 14, 21, 24, 36, 41, 42, 70, 89; *Framework for School Inspection* 16; student development survey 51–2
Oldham, England, and deprivation 44
Oliver, J.E. 43
openness of schools 35–8
Orthodox schools 25, 39, 52–3, 56; and community cohesion 58, 86, 107; *see also* anti-Semitism
Ouseley report 40, 100

Parekh, B. 7, 100
parents: and diversity (Jewish) 52; and engagement 55–6, 76; and fear (Muslims') 73; parental choice 8–11, 15, 29, 39, 45–6, 58, 69, 106, 108
Parker-Jenkins, M. 11, 13, 24, 25, 30, 46, 56–7, 65, 66, 67, 69, 80, 85–6, 87, 103, 106
Pearce, S. 13
Pellegrino, J.W. 90
Phillips, T. 99, 105
Pikuach reports 24, 53, 86
PISA (Programme for International Student Assessment) 93
private education 9, 29, 38
Protestantism, and education 26–9, 36, 45
public education 10, 17, 29, 30, 33, 36–8
Pugh, G. 7, 66
purdah 69
Putnam, R.D. 32

race: definition 7; and multiculturalism 101–2; *see also* discrimination; hostility
Race Relations Act 39, 104
racism 43, 56–7, 59, 76, 80, 103, 106; *see also* bullying
recruitment: of students 53–4; of teachers 21–2
Reform Judaism 53
Richardson, R. 71, 99
Rizvi, S. 46–7
Robbins, M. 24, 109
Rowe, D. 14, 41
Runnymede Trust 10, 78

Sacks, J. 7, 8, 54–5
safety *see* security
Said, E. 76
salvation doctrine 35
Sarwar, G. 72, 85
School Standards and Framework Act (1998) 20, 21
Schools: Building on success (DfEE) 11
Scotland 26–7
sectarianism 28, 34, 38, 45–6, 70
secular education 19, 36; in France 29–32, 69; and multiculturalism 101–2

139

security: and Islamophobia 74–5, 77–9; in Jewish schools 56, 57, 59–62; in Muslim schools 69–70, 76–7
segregation 5, 8, 34–6; and community engagement 40, 42, 72–3, 80, 89; in Northern Ireland 27–8; and parental choice 9; and self-exclusion 12, 56, 58, 99
Sephardi Jews 23, 53
Sevita, V. 9, 13, 15, 73, 89, 107–8
Shain, F. 71, 102
Shuayb, M. 38
Simpson, L. 68–9, 74, 81, 92, 99, 102, 106, 109–10
skill development: '3 Ts' model 92; assessment programmes 93–4; deep learning model 90; definition of 91–2; 'well-educated' formula 92, 93
social capital: and bonding 7, 32, 67; and community cohesion 15, 44, 55, 89, 98; and skill development 91
state-funded schools 15, 18–19, 21, 23, 25, 27, 29, 33–4, 49, 50–1, 66; *see also* independent schools
Statham, J. 14, 15
sustainability, cultural 2, 5, 10, 23, 96
synagogues 22, 49–50, 52–3, 54

tarfqa 67
teachers: and community cohesion 54–5, 58, 76, 86; and hostility 78, 56–7, 59–62; and security 69, 74–5, 77; selection and training 21–2, 27, 50—1, 52, 66, 94; and skill development 92–3
teaching material 51
Telhaj, S. 7, 66
terrorism: and community cohesion 74; and multiculturalism 102, 105; and xenophobia 77, 79

texts (sacred), and community preservation 51
tolerance 7, 10, 108, 110; and identity 20, 36–7, 73; and skill development 90, 92; and segregation 15, 34, 89
Tony Blair Faith Foundation 94
trust: and community cohesion 12, 38, 43, 76, 107; and engagement 84–5

ummah 8, 67, 72
uniforms *see* clothing
United States, openness of Catholic schools 36–7, 45

VA (Voluntary Aided) schools 11, 15, 19, 25
Varshney, A. 88
voluntary controlled schools 19, 25
voluntary schools 19

Wales: history of religious schools 17–19; schooling legislation 19–22
Walford, G. 25, 28, 29, 65
Weller, P. 59, 75, 77
Werbner, P. 7, 59, 67, 81, 99, 107
West-Burnham, J. 15, 58, 84, 90
Wood, A. 71

xenophobia 57, 59, 60, 77, 79; *see also* anti-Semitism; bullying; Islamophobia

Yeshiva schools 4
Young, J. 43, 100
Yuval-Davis, N. 26, 104